GET
UN
STUCK

GET UN STUCK

Stop stressing about money and get ahead faster

BEN NASH

WILEY

Disclaimer
The material in this publication is of the nature of general comment only, and does not represent professional advice. It is not intended to provide specific guidance for particular circumstances and it should not be relied on as the basis for any decision to take action or not take action on any matter which it covers. Readers should obtain professional advice where appropriate, before making any such decision. To the maximum extent permitted by law, the author and publisher disclaim all responsibility and liability to any person, arising directly or indirectly from any person taking or not taking action based on the information in this publication.

For Yang

Contents

About the author

If you're not familiar with me or Pivot Wealth, you might be wondering who I am and why I'm the best person to help you Get Unstuck.

I'm a financial adviser and the founder of Pivot Wealth, a money management company that helps people invest smarter to create a life not limited by money. I'm deeply passionate about helping people make better money choices so they can live a better life.

Through my work I draw on my practical experience to simplify the often overwhelming area of money by distilling complex tactics and strategies into simple, practical, actionable steps. I'm also a speaker, podcaster, writer, TikTok'er, financial educator, a regular writer for News.com.au, and author of the book *Replace Your Salary by Investing*.

My content is authentic, practical, to the point, and jargon-free to drive rapid implementation and rapid results.

Unlike the majority of Financial Advisers in Australia I've chosen to focus on people in their 30s and 40s still building their wealth towards financial independence. Also in contrast to traditional financial advice, my work has a strong focus on lifestyle alongside money outcomes, something I feel is crucial to drive a money plan that will actually work for you.

I'm a finance geek at heart and have studied extensively in the area of finance including two Master's degrees and my undergraduate study, alongside a number of specific financial advice professional qualifications. That being said, it's primarily through my practical experience that the concepts in this book are drawn from.

Both myself and Pivot Wealth have been formally recognised, named as part of the Financial Standard Top 50 most Influential Financial Advisers in Australia for six consecutive years, the Independent Financial Adviser Industry Thought Leader of the Year, Innovator of the Year (twice), Association of Financial Advisers Excellence in Education Award, Best Client Servicing Financial Adviser in Australia, Best Client Servicing Financial Advice Firm, Marketing Program of the Year, and Pivot Wealth has been listed as part of the Australian Financial Review's 100 Fastest Growing Companies in Australia. We have also been recognised as award finalists for Wellness Program of the Year, Self Licensed Firm of the Year, Digital Advice Strategy of the Year, Women's Community Program of the Year, SME Employer of the Year, and part of the AFR Boss Best Places to Work.

I've partnered with leading organisations to deliver financial education content, including working with the National Rugby League (NRL) to create and deliver their financial education program for all professional male and female NRL players. In addition, we've delivered content for the Australian Government, Newscorp, Glaxosmith Kleine, WeWork, Pearler, SelfWealth, Raiz Invest, VoltBank, Work-Shop, and Publicis Media, among others.

In addition to my work at Pivot, I'm a co-founder of Ensombl, Australia's biggest community of Financial Advisers dedicated to driving the positive evolution of Financial Advice in Australia and around the world.

Having advised and coached over a thousand people directly through one-on-one financial advice, worked indirectly with thousands more, and presented to over 100 000 people through live events, I've found what really works (and what doesn't).

When you have a solid understanding of what's really possible you become empowered to confidently make the smartest money choices. The feeling of being empowered, the relief that comes from knowing your money is sorted, and the elimination of money stress is something I passionately believe every person should have and something I feel very privileged to help people achieve.

Acknowledgements

Firstly, I want to thank my three favourite women. My wife Yang, for her constant, ongoing support. My mum, for giving me the confidence and belief to make this book happen. And my nan, for giving me the book that started my passion for personal finance.

I'd also like to thank my amazing mentors and coaches. Mark Power, for showing me the ropes. Dean Holmes, for helping me to launch my business and teaching me how to do advice right. Steve Salvia, for helping me to clarify my message and create a service that connects with people. Andrew Griffiths and David Dugan for giving me the framework and motivation to make this book actually happen.

Huge thanks to my Ensombl Co-Founders Clayton Daniel, Ray Jaramis and Adrian Patty, for bringing together an amazing community that I've been so lucky to learn from over the last four years.

And finally, thanks to all the other amazing advisers who've shared their knowledge with me for the benefit of financial advice, in particular the broader Ensombl and AFA communities. There are too many of you to name but you know who you are. All the best things I've learned have come from you: thank you *so* much for sharing.

Preface

When writing *Get Unstuck*, there were two key areas I felt people needed to know to nail it with their money.

Firstly, I wanted to help people understand the psychology, decision-making, and thinking that drives real money success—and how you can shift your own thinking to make it easier to get better results with the money you have today.

This resulted in my diving deep into the rabbit hole of behavioural finance and money psychology, so I could pull out the most important principles and simplify them into the actionable steps you can take to make money easier.

Unfortunately, you're not naturally set up for success when it comes to saving and investing, which is why so many people struggle to come anywhere close to achieving their financial potential.

But it doesn't have to be this way.

When you understand enough of how your thinking works around saving and investing, it becomes a lot easier to 'hack your thinking' and set yourself up for success. Helping you understand the key things you need to know to do exactly this is the first step in true money success, which is why I made this the first focus for *Get Unstuck*.

The second element I wanted to unpack was the foundational money management, saving, and investing systems you should be using if you want to get maximum results in the shortest amount of time *without* taking on crazy or unnecessary risks.

Through *Get Unstuck* I outline the core systems I use for my own saving, planning, and investing, and the exact same systems I've helped thousands of others set up to help them create a life not limited by money.

Success with money is simple; you need to spend less than you earn, and invest as much money as possible, as intelligently as possible — this is what will deliver you the best results from whatever you have to work with.

But simple doesn't mean easy.

The practical application of these 'success ingredients' is *hard*. It's hard because there are so many options, too much information, and your money success in the *future* is in direct conflict with your wants and needs *today*.

Having the right systems in place makes your work here easier.

Through this book, my aim is to help you create the mindset you need for true money success, understand the thinking you need to make it actually happen, and build the systems that will deliver the results you want from your money.

Money can be overwhelming. There are so many things you *could* do, and so much you feel like you need to know and learn, figuring out what to do next can seem almost impossible. But what most people don't realise is that you don't need to know everything about money now, you just need to know enough to take your next step.

Once you take that step, you learn things and build skills that make the steps that come next 1) clearer and 2) easier. This book is all about helping you understand your next step and then giving you the confidence to take it.

There's some work to be done, but the results are worth it.

Introduction

My interest in money started by chance the day my nan gave me a book. The book was *Rich Dad, Poor Dad* by Robert Kiyosaki, and I was drawn to the simplicity with which Kiyosaki explained financial concepts I'd previously found confusing.

This book sparked an interest, and I'm a bit of a reader—so I started buying up all the personal finance books I could get my hands on. Shortly afterwards, I decided to go back to uni and study finance. That led to a graduate role in a traditional 'blue chip' money management company that helped rich people get richer.

I enjoyed the work: every day was different. I got to work with some interesting high-profile peeps, and everything went along swimmingly. Then, a few years later, I left that company to join a small business in the Sydney CBD that focused on working with first home buyers.

When I started in the industry, I'd enjoyed helping people use the rules to keep more of their money. But there's something slightly more rewarding about helping people buy their first home and set up their family's (or potential family's) future than there is about helping some super-rich dude save $200k in tax so he can buy a bigger boat.

I joined this small business to build their financial advice arm, so I went to work creating a service that would be valuable to people in their 20s and 30s. I asked our clients about the problems they were facing; and, while everyone's situation was unique, I definitely saw some common themes in their problems, including:

- Being overwhelmed by too many options and too much information
- Not being able to effectively balance financial success and enjoy an epic lifestyle at the same time
- Being time-poor and not wanting to waste their precious spare time doing something they weren't good at and didn't enjoy

They didn't know what information was important or what to do with the information they had. They were scared of doing the wrong thing, so they did…NOTHING!

It's so easy to fall into what I call 'the inaction trap' with money. Most financial benefits only come from taking ACTION. So if you fall into this trap, you end up missing the opportunity to get your income, savings and investments all working harder for you and moving you closer to the lifestyle you want.

Once I recognised this, I created a financial planning and advice service to help people solve these problems. I'd look at their income and spending, plus what was left over and their existing assets, and help them to create a strategy for putting their money to work. The output was a plan that showed them the path from where they were that day to the money (and non-money) results they wanted.

And when I first started doing this, I looked at the numbers and got *really* excited.

I could see that my plan gave my clients the potential to very quickly grow their savings, investments and assets. I was stoked. They were going to grow some epic cash over time, which meant they could live a great lifestyle.

Then, when I showed my clients the plan, I could see their excitement build as they imagined all the things they could do with this cash. I asked them about the difference this money would make to them, and they started telling me about all the things they wanted to do. The epic trips overseas. The ability to look after their parents. The flexibility around their work. And the list went on.

I told them how much they'd need to save to make the plans happen, and what to do with their savings to get the results in their plan. Then I normally suggested we book in another check-in with them in six months' time.

In the month before the first check-in was scheduled, I found myself imagining the meetings in my mind. I pictured big congratulations, high fives, maybe even a bear hug or two. I figured my clients would be so happy with their progress — from saving almost nothing to crushing it — that they might even consider naming their firstborn after me.

That *wasn't* what happened.

I still remember the first meeting. As the clients came into the office and I greeted them, there were no high fives. The clients were fairly quiet, though, so I just chalked it up to personality.

When we sat down, I was all smiles. They, however, weren't. In fact, they looked nervous and a little upset. Definitely no bear hugs or offers to name their children after me. And when I asked the clients how they were going, they said, 'Not well.'

Concerned, I asked more questions; and they went on to tell me about the long list of things that had 'come up' and stopped them getting the results they needed. It felt like a confessional. I could tell my clients were frustrated.

Then, when I looked at the numbers, I could see my clients weren't on track. They weren't even close. They'd increased their savings a tiny bit, but also increased spending on credit. Overall, they'd gone BACKWARDS. I was shocked.

We talked about the impact of this setback, and I showed them the disastrous effect that continuing on this path would have on their original plan. They weren't happy, but they told me that these issues were one-off exceptions, and wouldn't be an ongoing thing.

So we reset their strategy and targets, and confirmed what they'd need to do over the next six months to get back on track. By the end of the meeting, my clients were feeling much better, and they left once again pumped up to go out and get their planned results.

This was only my first review meeting, so I figured it was a one-off. But, over more and more meetings, I discovered that the majority of my clients *also* weren't on track. They all had similar stories about what had come up to stop them sticking to the plan we'd set. Their reasons were different: little Jimmy needed special shoes, they had an 'emergency' getaway to reduce stress levels, or they NEEDED a new wood-fire pizza oven for their house. But very few of my clients had hit the targets they'd set for themselves.

In fact, only one person had managed it: an actuary who was already pretty good with money and just needed help to get to the next level. This client was all over it. Most, however, weren't.

I got quite concerned at this point: both for my clients, and for the advice I was giving. I had no interest in helping people build awesome plans that never actually came together. So I started trying to figure out why this had happened, and what I could do to fix it.

I came up with a few questions and started asking my clients for feedback. Pretty much all of them told me that they knew what to do, but actually doing it was hard work. They were spending a bunch of time trying to manage their money, but it was going everywhere. They were constantly 'juggling' money from one place to another, and pushing to get the results they'd planned for.

Because there was so much work, they lost motivation over time and just gave up. I asked what would make getting results easier, and the feedback was almost unanimous. People needed a structured process to make it easy to save and invest their money the way they'd planned.

Now we were getting somewhere.

I'm a process nut. I think that with enough thought and attention, most things in life can be broken down into a clear, easy-to-follow process. Creating these sorts of processes is one of my strengths, so I went to work creating a spending, saving and banking system to make money management easy.

It took a lot of effort to get there: almost five years of tweaking and refining the process. But the results speak for themselves. The recent statistics I've pulled on my clients' savings show that people who follow this process save—on average—over 35 per cent of their income. That's more than *seven times* the Australian national savings average of 4.7 per cent.

And the impact? As you'll learn through this book, the power of time and money is a beautiful thing. If the average 30-year-old saved this much extra income and invested it, they'd have an additional $3.4m by age 60.

I believe that every single person should be able to live 'a life not limited by money'. But if you're like most young people today, this isn't easy. You want it all without sacrificing anything. You want a life that fulfils you and makes you happy. And you can have one.

How? Having that life means realising that money doesn't solve problems, but it *does* create options. Those options empower you with choices to do the things you want and live the life you want. Because, unless your dream life is living off the land in a forest or jungle somewhere, you need money to make it possible.

Again, it's not easy. Writing this book took me down a rabbit hole of complexities, options and choices around saving, investing, property, insurance and money in general. It was overwhelming.

There are tens of thousands of investment options just in Australia, and hundreds of thousands across global markets. And that's just investments. There are even more options for banking, retirement, property, and other investments and financial products. And then you have the strategy options. Pay down debt, contribute to super, buy shares, don't buy shares, invest overseas, buy property, don't buy property...you get the picture.

How do you choose which is best for you? Which combination of strategies, investments and products will get you what YOU want? Making this choice is difficult even for people who work in finance or money management.

Add to this the pressure we (and social media) place on ourselves to 'keep up' with our peers, and our personal and professional networks. The icing on the cake is our inbuilt psychology and decision-making processes, which work entirely against us when it comes to money. And then there's the barrage of advice we get from mates, family and our friendly Uber drivers.

Everyone has a different opinion about what you should do with your money. They tell you to buy shares, buy property, don't buy property, contribute to your super fund, and it goes on...each person is entirely convinced that they're suggesting the absolute best thing to do, and that everyone else is wrong.

No wonder you end up confused.

Sadly, there's no silver bullet. I speak to a lot of people about money, and they often ask questions like, 'I've got $10k and I want to do something smart with it. What should I do?' I've actually lost count of the number of times I've heard this exact question.

Unfortunately for all of us, there *is* no one right answer to this question. There's no one pathway that will always deliver the best results. The right answer is different for everyone. The best thing for you depends on where you are now, what you want to do over time, and what's important to you. This book was written to help you understand how to figure out what YOUR best pathway is.

Because, while there's no one pathway that can guarantee money success for everyone, there are things that everyone should know about money. There are also tools and concepts that everyone needs to understand to know how to make smart choices that are right for them.

And that's what you'll learn as you work through this book.

The importance of education

I've got a lot of teachers in my family. My mum was a primary school teacher; and from a young age, she drilled the importance of education into me.

I must have listened to her, because one of my true pleasures in life is learning. I've done a bunch of formal study, and I'm still learning every single day. That learning comes both through running and growing my financial planning business Pivot Wealth, and through the financial advice, planning and coaching work I do with my clients. That's why, whether you focus on your work, health, money, or any other area, I think educating yourself is so important.

When you understand your options and know what you should be doing, everything becomes easier. You can kick butt in your job. You can become healthier and live longer. You can pursue the interests you care about. And you can make it easier to get your money sorted.

It doesn't matter which path you take to reach your version of money success, you still need to educate yourself.

Education lets you choose the best options to get you the results you want. It helps you to build confidence in your strategy and direction. A solid understanding allows you to reduce and manage risk. And maybe most importantly, it helps you to stick with your strategy when you should; or change, adjust or refine what you're doing when needed.

I can help *anyone* create a money strategy that will get them awesome results. But if I don't educate them about why the strategy is so good, or how it will work for them, they're much less likely to get the results we planned for.

If you don't have enough knowledge about the 'why' behind your strategy, you'll forget why you're doing whatever you're doing. A colleague will tell you how they made big money following some interesting financial strategy, and your ears will prick up. You'll wonder whether that option might be better for you. It'll sound better—and without enough education, you won't fully understand why you're on your current path.

Then you'll get distracted by these 'shiny objects', and get off track.

So regardless of the money path you choose, you need to educate yourself to clearly understand why it's good for you. You should also understand why you're NOT doing any of the multitude of other things you could possibly do with your cash.

Invest in your money education, and it will pay benefits for years to come. Not only in the financial benefits, but in time saved as you avoid distractions, confidence in your strategy, and less money-related stress.

The three money areas you HAVE to get right

My past experiences with clients have led me to think about what the critical elements of money success actually are.

I've found there are three key areas you need to get right to be successful with money. These three areas are all related, and they work together. If any one of them is missing or not up to scratch, you'll never achieve true success with money. The three areas are **Structure**, **Strategy** and **Solutions**.

Structure

Your **Structure** is how you manage your money on a day-to-day basis. The biggest part of this is your spending, saving and banking habits. Your money psychology and decision-making processes have a huge—and enormously underestimated—impact on the results you get with money.

So you need to be aware of your flawed thinking and biases to avoid their impact.

If you know the steps involved and what to look for, you can make your money management psychology work for you instead of against you. To help with this, I'm going to step you through your money psychology and biases in the first three chapters. Then, in the fourth chapter, I'll show you how to put this knowledge into practice to make managing your money simple and effective.

The results of getting this right are powerful. They flow through to *all* other areas of your money and (should) drive the choices you're making. You need to know how much money you need for spending now, and how much you can direct to making smart choices for the future—e.g. investing, or saving for a rainy day or emergencies.

Then, once you're on top of your spending and saving, you're all set to get smart and make your money work harder for you.

However, most people skim over this area, dishing out the good old Aussie 'She'll be right' strategy. They might write a loose budget that they never really stick to, or download an app that tells them how much they've spent after the fact.

Neither of these options allows you to confidently take action, however. And if you try any sort of investing, property buying, or other strategy before you're solid on your savings numbers, you could be setting yourself up for failure. For example, if you need to access money you've put into an investment or strategy at a non-ideal time (like when investment markets are down), you could be forced to sell or withdraw cash and lose money in the process.

Getting on top of your spending, saving and banking first will allow you to make smart choices from a position of confidence.

Strategy

There are no 'universally good' money choices. There are only choices. Some will be good for you. Others won't. It's common today to get advice and information from different sources who swear by one particular strategy, investment or financial solution. This can lead you to think there's some magical money pathway that's right for everyone.

Unfortunately, it's just not that easy.

There are always different options that can get you to your money and non-money 'wants'. Some will get you there faster with more risk. Others might mean slower progress but less risk. Some options will make you uncomfortable. Others will just feel 'right' for you.

A good strategy will help you choose the path that's right for you.

When you're making money choices, it's common to face fear. Actually, fear is common in *all* areas of life, but it can be a big barrier to getting positive money results.

Fear is completely natural, and at the right time, it can stop you from doing the wrong thing. But it can also be paralysing. Unless you have a way to push through it and get to a point of confidence that a money choice is either good (and you should do it), or bad (and you should avoid it), you end up stuck in the inaction trap.

A good strategy will allow you to push through fear so you can take action with confidence.

Setting goals also forms part of your strategy and helps you to be money-smart. Without goals, you're just making sacrifices with no real upside. It's also almost impossible to get the most out of your money without clear targets. If you try, you're likely to get off track, or worse, give up all together.

When you set goals, though, you reframe your thinking. You're motivated by remembering the results you'll get when you stick to your strategy. This makes your life easier, and drastically increases your chances of money success.

Solutions

When I talk about solutions, what I'm referring to are the investments and product solutions you use to grow your assets and income over time.

But when most people start trying to sort out their money, they immediately think about investing. They want to grow their savings and assets, so they look for an investment solution to make them some sweet cash money.

They hear the stories of Facebook, Google, Apple and other share investments that have grown quickly and made a bunch of people rich in the process. They hear about the baby boomers who've made millions buying properties in 'hotspots' that increased ten times in value, so they could retire with the sweetest caravan money could buy and join the grey nomads travelling the country.

These stories lead them to think they can retire at 25, stacking dollar bills and day trading in their underwear.

But, as I mentioned above, starting with investments is backwards. It can cause you to make investment choices that are inconsistent with everything else you're trying to achieve from a money and non-money perspective.

Instead, your investment and financial product solutions should naturally flow from your overall money strategy or plan. Setting a smart strategy first will help you get clear on the sorts of investments that will deliver the results you want.

Besides, as you'll learn through this book, the day trading strategy doesn't work for most people. Chances are high that it won't work for you because it involves more risk than you need to take to get the results you want. You don't need to shoot the lights out with every investment. And you can't.

The investments and product solutions you choose should be ones that best get you from where you are now to the results you want in the future. And the step most people miss is that your solutions should get you there with the LOWEST amount of risk possible. You should have a balanced approach that reduces (or ideally eliminates) the chances of serious loss and momentum-killing setbacks.

And if you know what to look for, these solutions are much easier to find.

When you're smart about the solutions you use, you'll build confidence in your overall strategy and the direction you're headed. Choosing solutions that support your strategy will help you avoid those 'shiny object' distractions and psychological biases that can lead you off-track and prompt mistakes.

In the third section of this book we'll cover the most effective investment and product solutions that you need to understand. Once you're across these key areas, you'll have the final piece of the money puzzle, and you'll be all set to get the results you want when you take action.

Ideas without action are meaningless

I've written this book to help you understand the key areas you need to get right to achieve money success. In it, I've covered the most important things you need to be aware of and consider when setting up your money to get the results you want. You'll also learn the key questions you need to ask to make truly smart choices and avoid the common money mistakes that can hold you back.

I'm going to give you a bunch of new ideas that can help you get better money results. But to get any benefit out of reading this book, you *need* to take action. As with anything important, you need to ACT to get results.

It's so common for people to get caught up in day-to-day cares, and neglect their money without giving the future much thought. If you do this, however, you'll remain 'stuck' forever, and will eventually have to settle for a much worse lifestyle than what's really possible.

I've designed this book to empower you to *take* that action. I want to give you the knowledge, tools and motivation you need to get started. Taking action is the most important thing you can do to drive money success.

But, like anything worthwhile, this won't just happen on its own. By picking up this book you've made the choice to get started on that journey, and I want to congratulate you for that. I hope this is your first step in getting 'unstuck'.

And more than that, I hope you enjoy it.

—Ben

SECTION 1
STRUCTURE

When you have complete confidence in the strategy and direction you're taking with your money, everything else becomes easy. And a good 'structure' for your money management is the first step to building this confidence.

When I say 'structure', I mean the way your money actually works on a day-to-day basis. Putting a solid structure in place gives you full confidence in what you do with your money day-to-day. You know what you have to work with, which then allows you to plan smart and make better investment choices: topics we cover in Sections 2 and 3 of this book.

Through this section, I'm going to help you build that solid structure. And I know from working with people one on one that you need knowledge to get there. So I'm going to go through the theory (Chapters 1-3) and then bring it all together in the practical (Chapter 4) to help you understand why this all works, as well as how.

As I mentioned in the Introduction, the biggest parts of your money structure are your income, spending and banking. When you're young, money in vs money out (and what's left over) is the biggest driver of your money results.

Through my financial advice and coaching work, I've noticed that people find saving money is hard. I mean *really* hard. As I write this, I can feel a rant coming on, but we'll get into why later in this section so I won't get started now…

What I will say is that I've found saving is much harder without a good system and process (structure) to manage your money.

So, by the end of this section, I'm going to show you how to create a simple but highly effective money management structure. I'll show you a banking system that makes it easier to save more money, while still spending guilt-free on the things you value most.

And while I do, I want to give you the confidence to take the action needed to set the system up, and then follow through to create real results.

It's common when people start thinking about money to want to jump into the sexy stuff: investing, buying property, and creating complex and expensive tax structures. PLEASE DON'T DO THIS.

Setting up a good structure will make everything else money-related easy. Take the time to get this right, and you'll find it easy to save, plan like a total boss, and make better investment choices. You'll also avoid the most common money mistakes that hold people back.

As I wrote this section, I unleashed my inner money nerd and dived deep into money psychology and decision-making. This is important stuff, because understanding WHY you behave the way you do (and what you can do to avoid your biases and bad behaviour) gives you a big advantage when you're setting up your money. So I also want to take you through the most important things you need to know about money psychology and decision-making.

This was my favourite part of the book to write and research, so I hope you enjoy reading it as much as I enjoyed writing it.

See you on the other side …

CHAPTER 1

Don't think yourself poor

I worked with a client—let's call her Lola—for a few years.

Lola was a successful young executive who'd fallen into a bit of a debt cycle. When we met, she was super-stressed. She'd let one debt roll into another, and accumulated a few more on the way.

Lola also had a lot of different things going on with her money management. She was very effective in her job. She was smart, motivated and generally results-driven. But for some reason she couldn't clearly identify, she just couldn't get the money results she wanted.

I spent some time with her talking through how she managed her money and what she'd done in the past, to identify what had gone wrong. We also spoke about the results that were most important to her.

At that point, I started noticing a trend. Lola kept self-sabotaging.

That surprised me initially, because Lola was a great planner. She had an *epic* to-do list, which she used religiously. At work, she was all about progress measures and KPIs. And she'd put together a strategy to solve her money issues that looked great on paper.

But when it came to doing the doing, the results just weren't happening.

I asked Lola how she actually implemented her plan, and how her money 'worked' in practice; and she started listing out the steps involved. On payday, money came into Account 1, and she transferred a proportion over to Account 2, which she used to pay for certain expenses. Then there was another account to pay a different debt, another transfer to a different bank to clear her credit card, a calculation of what was coming up and what was left over, a review of two other debts to establish how much of the leftover money to pay to them, and a manual payment to cover something else…

She kept talking and her list went on.

In her job, Lola often worked to tight deadlines, and critical issues regularly came up that needed immediate responses. Lola handled it all well, but her job commitments and career ambition meant her work regularly required all her attention, and everything else took a back seat.

This is completely normal for many people, and doesn't mean you can't be successful with money. Lola's problem was that her money management process had so many manual steps that she just didn't have enough time to make it happen. So her plan fell apart.

The lesson? If you're time-poor, or like most people just don't enjoy spending your spare time managing money, DON'T set up a strategy that requires loads of your time input.

A good money management strategy works smoothly and easily, flowing without taking up all your spare time. It's also easy to understand, so you're clear on what needs doing when — and why.

But with the way most people manage their money today, this isn't as easy as it sounds. I've lost count of the number of people I've spoken to who've tried to get better results from their money, only to run into a roadblock (sometimes more than one).

It's no wonder they get frustrated and give up.

I used to think this was because they didn't know all the rules. But now I know there are other factors at play. The more research I do, the more I realise how hard it is to be naturally

To get the results you want from money, you need a secret weapon.

successful with money. I now know that to get the results you want from money, you need a secret weapon. You need a head start — some kind of performance enhancer.

Unfortunately, our inbuilt human thinking, tendencies and biases stack the odds against us when it comes money management.

Plus, today it's easier than ever before to spend money without thinking. Paypass, Apple Pay, recurring subscriptions, opt-outs, free trials (which then cost $19.95 per month), software as a service...the list goes on.

I even recently got a new watch that allows me to pay for stuff. A WATCH.

It's like there's a global conspiracy to make us poor.

Our money-related behaviours intrigue many people (myself included). In fact, many people who are much smarter than me have dedicated their careers to understanding money-related decision-making and psychology.

I did a lot of research as I wrote this book — and the more I do, the more I realise how much decision-making and psychology influence how we manage our money. They also impact our results and chances of success. My research has shown me why the way most people manage their money makes it difficult to get the results they want.

To be truly successful with money, you need to 'hack' your thinking. You need to make your money psychology work *for* you, instead of against you. You need to structure your money management to give yourself the best chance of getting the results you want. And you can't do that unless you know how you're making money decisions.

So, throughout this chapter, we'll cover the key decision-making and psychology processes that have the biggest influence on your money management. I want to help you understand what these factors are and how you can use them to your advantage. This is the area of money that will have the largest impact on your results, so lean in and listen close...

We're all time-poor

Time is precious: it's the most valuable resource any of us have. We can use that time to enjoy experiences, build relationships with the important people in our lives and make money, or we can spend it chain-watching random TV series on Netflix.

Today we're more time-poor than *ever* before. Young professionals, in particular, work longer hours and have less leisure time than ever before. And because they're paid more today than in the past, their time is worth more.

If that describes you, then you don't want to waste the precious little spare time you have doing things you don't enjoy. And that's true for all areas of your life.

Of course, there are important things in life that aren't enjoyable. It's important to go to the dentist, have regular health checks, and pay your bills. But, if you're like most people, you'd rather spend your time doing something else.

So, because your time is limited, it makes sense to minimise the amount you spend on these things. In other words, when you're doing an important-but-not-enjoyable activity, you should aim to get the best possible outcome from it while minimising your time input.

And for most people, money management falls into this category.

So the more time a strategy requires you to spend managing your money, the less likely you are to stick to it. The more time-consuming sticking to your strategy is, the more likely you are to get off-track. If you're time-poor and don't enjoy crunching numbers in spreadsheets or juggling money around 13 different bank accounts, you'll get frustrated.

As a result, you just give up — or at least stop giving your money management the attention it needs to get the results you want.

That's why the most effective money management approach is often the one that demands the least amount of your time. A 'low-touch', less time-intensive strategy frees up more of your valuable time to spend on other things.

The most effective money management approach is often the one that demands the least amount of your time.

And more free time isn't the only benefit to a low-touch money management strategy. It will also get you more of the results you want, because it doesn't rely on you finding extra time (that you don't have) to make it work. This in turn allows you to set success as your default. It lets you hit the magic 'autopilot' button, so everything flows in the background as you make steady, constant progress.

Thankfully for Lola, this wasn't the first time I'd seen her problem. So she and I spent some time talking through all the different financial inputs like income, savings ability, assets, debts, goals and targets, etc. Then, together, we designed an AUTOMATED money management system for her.

Once we hit the 'go' button on this system, everything just happened. She could get on with her work and whatever else was important to her, knowing that what she wanted to happen with her money was actually happening.

And she's been kicking butt ever since.

So what can you learn from Lola? Unless you make a conscious effort to streamline your finance setup, it's easy for your money management to get out of control.

I see so many people who accumulate bank accounts, random financial products, apps and spreadsheets to 'help' them manage their money better. Over time, their personal finances become so complex that they hardly know where everything actually is, let alone where it should be. This makes it difficult to get everything working together and heading in the same direction.

Instead, simplify, streamline and automate as much of your money management as possible. You'll get to spend less time managing money, free up more time for the things you really enjoy, and give you a better chance of getting the results you want.

Simplify, streamline and automate as much of your money management as possible.

That's a big part of what I mean when I talk about putting a solid structure around your money. It's extremely powerful but often overlooked.

Stick to the defaults

People generally stick to what's easiest. We like the simple path.

We get caught up in everything that's happening around us—the (seemingly) urgent things—and neglect anything that's important but not urgent. Things like curating Spotify playlists, looking at cat photos on Instagram and replying to emails seem critical, so we focus on them.

And we often get a sense of satisfaction and immediate pleasure from these things, but they add little true value to our lives.

I've seen this too many times to count when I meet new people in my Financial Advice and Coaching work. For a long time, I questioned why this happens. I've often become frustrated watching people neglect important things like money management to focus on random things that have much less impact on their lives.

I met a couple a while back who perfectly illustrated this. Let's change their names to protect the innocent and call them Liam and Chloe.

Liam and Chloe were a lovely couple, and we got on really well. They were both young professionals in their mid-30s who worked in advertising, and had high-profile jobs with very healthy six-figure incomes. They'd recently had their first child, and enjoyed living a great lifestyle, travelling regularly, eating out at nice restaurants, dressing well and collecting the latest tech toys.

They worked hard for their money (as expected at that income level); and while they could save a lot of money each month, they had no real direction with their finances. They hadn't taken the time to focus on the goals that were important to them, so they'd experienced a lot of 'leakage' as a result.

That meant they didn't have much to show for the ten years they'd each been earning those healthy incomes. They'd regularly saved a little (relative to their incomes), but had no other investments. And they didn't want to work at the pace they were currently going at forever. Ideally, they wanted to be able to wind back from work before they reached age 50.

When we met and talked through their situation, I could see a huge opportunity. They could continue living a great lifestyle and ALSO direct a healthy chunk of their income towards making smart choices that would start setting up the future lifestyle they wanted.

I thought through their options, and I could see plenty.

For example, when we first met, Liam and Chloe recognised that they hadn't taken advantage of the income they'd earned to date. They were motivated to take action, so I explained my approach to helping people make smarter money choices, and they loved it.

They hated spending what little spare time they had managing their money, so they could see how this process would get them results. They could also see how it would help them change some of their behaviours, and easily help them save much more than they'd managed in the past.

So they agreed to get this moving.

Their next step was to book in three meetings with me over the next month to work through their issues and set up their plan. Their work would be minimal: all they really needed to do was turn up, gather a small amount of information, and make some choices. I'd do the rest.

Liam and Chloe both told me they were ready, and that they'd work out their schedules and come back to me. I was happy for them and excited to help.

Then, however, they contacted me a couple of times after our meeting to tell me that work issues had come up. They wanted to move forward, but were waiting for the right time. So, I waited.

A couple of months later, they contacted me again to say they still wanted to move ahead, but new things had come up that were stopping them. They said, 'Not now but soon.'

At this point, I started losing faith.

About a year later, I bumped into Liam at a function. Before I could speak, he jumped in and said that they still wanted to move ahead, but hadn't taken any action because they had been caught up with work. It was all just too hard right now, but they really planned to revisit their money management this year when they had 'less on their plates'.

I wasn't very confident.

Liam and Chloe had a set routine, which was to focus on their work, inbox, social events and whatever else they spent their little free time on. So their default around money was inconsistency and lack of structure. They had enough income to do this while spending pretty much whatever they wanted, but it meant they had little left over to save or invest.

In their book *Nudge*, Richard Thaler and Cass Sunstein talked about a ton of research they'd done around decision-making behaviour. This research confirmed that people strongly tend to stick to their default settings for many money-related choices.

Thaler and Sunstein did a study in the United States around retirement plans. In the US, people have to actually opt in to their employer's retirement scheme. The study found that when people had to opt in, the scheme's take-up rate (and associated savings) was only 65 per cent.

Many of the plans they looked at during this study involved an option where members didn't have to put in any of their own money. All they had to do was opt in to the scheme, and their employer would put FREE money into their retirement account on their behalf. But they didn't opt in.

That same study found that where enrolment in an employer's retirement scheme was automatic, the take-up rate increased to 98 per cent. That's a full one-third more people participating in their employer's retirement scheme when they were automatically opted in. All other plan details were exactly the same.

Why? Because people can be lazy. Well, actually, lazy isn't the right word. People can be highly motivated in other areas of their lives, but still inherently stick to default settings. They don't like to move offcourse, so they fall into a cycle of doing things in certain ways. This is even more evident in areas where there's no immediate outcome of their actions, for example losing weight, getting fit and healthy, studying for future career progression, or saving and investing money for the future.

Because these choices involve a distant future payoff, there's no immediate benefit. There's no sense of urgency or immediate pleasure hit. People's motivation to change their 'defaults' is reduced. Their state of inertia compounds. So they go back to the cat videos on YouTube (or other distractions), while promising themselves that they'll get to it 'soon'.

And then they suffer through poor results.

Most people don't save nearly as much as they need to live the lifestyle they want in the future. They don't put enough aside for coming things that they'll want to spend money on. They certainly don't save enough to allow retirement or winding back from work when they want to.

The average 30-year-old today will retire on less than 30 per cent of the average income, based on Australian saving statistics. They really want the things in the previous paragraph, but for some reason they don't prioritise or give those things the required (or deserved) effort and attention.

> **Most people don't save nearly as much as they need to live the lifestyle they want in the future.**

Liam and Chloe were a great example of this. They had their default money management setting, they were sticking with it.

Of course, I'm not saying you should neglect your career or use all your spare time managing money. On the contrary, as I said earlier, you want to minimise the time you spend on money management. And as a young professional, it's critical that you invest time and energy into progressing your career so you can grow your income over time.

And if you're thinking that you may as well just give up, set up the ultimate YouTube cat video playlist, and stuff your face with Uber Eats because you're doomed to failure, hold off. You might feel as though you've already been sabotaged by your inner human and that all hope is lost; but thankfully this isn't the case.

There *is* a solution. It's one that's worked for some of the rock star researchers, professors, and Nobel prize winners mentioned in this chapter, as well as for young professionals in practice. Following this proven process won't mean you completely avoid inertia, but it will get you positive results.

Your mindset won't totally change, but you'll avoid the problems created by your inbuilt tendencies. You'll still give in to your inner human, but you won't suffer the same consequences.

To make this work, you'll need to make an investment—not of money, but of time and attention. You'll have to 'hack' your thinking. And if you do, I promise your investment will pay for itself many times over.

Investing a small amount of time now to get your money management system right will set you up to make financial success your default result. This way you can still be human and stick to your default setting, while knowing that it will move you closer to the lifestyle and money results you want.

Once you set your strategy to make success your default, mucking it up will require going against your natural, inbuilt human tendencies. You'll have to actively step outside of your comfort zone to make a mistake. You'll have to breach your inbuilt drivers to **not** get the results you want.

You can do certain things around your saving, spending, investment planning, debt reduction strategy, and all the other areas of your money management to build success into your setup and hugely increase your chances of great results. And I'm going to show you *exactly* what those things are in the next three chapters.

We give in to temptation

We humans all want things to be as easy as possible. But there are cases when easiest is *not* best. In fact, sometimes, the easiest thing can cause a bunch of trouble.

For years, I've been meeting new people and talking about money. Most people I meet have a pretty good idea of what they want. They also know what they want to happen with their money on a day-to-day basis. But very few of them actually get these results.

And for a long time, I also struggled with this issue.

When I first started in the workforce after university, I was excited about what my new income could do for me. I thought about all the travel I could do. I figured I'd start steadily growing my small empire, building up investments and slowly-but-surely creating a fortune to rival Steve Jobs or Mark Zuckerberg.

First, I sat down and did a budget. I listed out all my fixed costs, including a healthy travel budget. Then I added in some pocket money for entertainment expenses and eating out. The numbers looked good, and I got excited thinking about the possibilities. Even after everything I wanted to spend my money on, I still had what I *thought* was a pretty healthy amount left over for saving.

But for some reason, every month, unexpected and unplanned things came up to throw me off. I needed a gift for a mate's birthday. Or I needed some tech for work. And of course, there was that weekend away that I HAD to have as a reward for working so hard.

Those things kept on coming. And the result? Well, it probably won't surprise you to hear that I didn't hit my savings targets. But the consequences were much worse than that. Not only did I miss my targets, but all those unplanned costs started eating into my holiday budget.

That made me sad: I didn't realise, at the time I spent my money, how much impact my choices would have on my ability to spend in other areas.

The funny thing is that if I'd had to choose between going to a mate's birthday party, having a weekend away, the new tech gear or taking that epic year-end trip to Europe, can you guess what I'd have picked? Granted, I liked all of those things. But travel is *much* more important to me, and I'd never knowingly sacrifice it for a bunch of little things.

Somehow, though, I did.

Brian Wansink is one of the pioneers of behavioural science and was previously a key contributor to the U.S. Government's nutrition policy.

In his book *Mindless Eating*, Wansink talked about a study he did on consumption behaviour with tomato soup. Half the study participants had a bowl of soup that continuously refilled from the bottom, while the rest had a regular bowl. Both groups were told to eat as much as they wanted.

Participants whose bowls refilled normally stopped eating far earlier, while those with never-ending soup often just kept eating until researchers eventually stopped the experiment.

Another of Wansink's studies involved moviegoers and five-day-old, stale popcorn. The popcorn was stale so researchers could ensure that it didn't actually appeal to participants.

Half of the participants were given a small container of popcorn, while the rest got a large container. The study found that those with the large container ate more than 53 per cent more popcorn on average than those with the smaller container.

Now you might be wondering what tomato soup and stale popcorn have to do with money. Fair question.

These two studies clearly show that you consume more when you have more. Whether it's tomato soup, stale popcorn or money, the bigger your 'serve', the more you'll mindlessly consume.

(It's worth noting here that Wansink is currently in hot water for alleged plagiarism [of himself—I'm not entirely sure how that works, but apparently it's quite a problem] and possible data misrepresentation issues. These issues apply to some of his other research, and don't affect the studies discussed above.)

Mindless consumption is especially frequent today in our age of abundance. You have access to more money than ever before. You've got a higher income, easier access to debt, and higher credit card limits than ever before. That means you need a 'hack' to reduce temptation.

Dilip Soman is a professor at the Rotman School of Management in Toronto. He's dedicated much of his career to researching consumer preferences and spending behaviour. Soman found that when we feel like we have more money, we spend more. But what's interesting is *how* this happens.

Soman found that when we spend money on credit, our 'mental accounting' (our internal tally of what we've spent) is flawed. When we spend on a credit card, we don't have to pay attention to how much we're spending. Because the limit on the card is much higher than what we'd normally spend, we don't need to think much about the actual amounts. And because we don't pay close attention, we tend to underestimate our spending. We round down without thinking, and we miss things.

The result is that we think we have more money than we actually do. And — as we've seen in the studies above — the more we think we have, the more we consume.

Soman conducted an experiment where a group of people replicated their spending behaviour. Half of the participants spent their money on credit, while the others used either cash or an account debit facility. The study then examined whether they'd spend any leftover money on a non-essential discretionary purchase.

The findings showed a direct link between spending on credit and the likelihood of buying the discretionary item.

Because these people had spent on credit without thinking, they had their mental accounting wrong, and they thought they had more money than they did. As a direct result, they tended to spend more on things they didn't really need.

And like the people in this study, my younger self had the best of intentions around my spending and saving, but I gave in to temptation. I was a sucker for it: that's why I spent most of my income on things I enjoyed in the moment, but didn't value as much as the things I REALLY wanted. I had money in easy reach, plus I spent on credit so I underestimated how much I'd spent.

Basically, I was drinking from the never-ending bowl of tomato soup.

Luckily, it didn't take me long to realise that I couldn't have it all. I had to make a choice. But I also figured out a few things I could do to make temptation easier to resist. I knew I had to set up my money management in a way that eliminated or reduced temptation wherever I could.

And I love a good hack—so I got to work creating a system (more on that below).

The power of barriers

I mentioned two of Brian Wansink's studies above, but I've saved the best for last. Wansink's flagship study looked at whether people were more likely to eat chocolates that were within easy reach and clearly visible versus ones that were still easily accessible (six feet away) and out of sight. Having the chocolate six feet away, of course, meant that eating it required standing up and taking approximately three steps.

In other words, it introduced a small barrier.

This small barrier caused a *huge* change in behaviour. Participants in the study who were six feet away from the chocolate ate less than half the amount compared to those who had them clearly in sight and within easy reach. **Less than half.**

In other words, small barriers between us and something that gives us pleasure change our behaviour. By requiring participants to stand up and take three steps to get to the chocolate, consumption was reduced by almost half. Small barriers have a big impact.

Small barriers have a big impact.

This effect applies to money as well. Putting the smallest of barriers between you and doing the wrong thing will have a massive impact on your behaviour (and your results).

An easy way to create these barriers is to have different bank accounts for different expenses. Even better is to have some of your accounts with different banks. This means you need to physically log into another bank and wait a day to blow your budget.

I implemented this small barrier within my personal banking a few years back, and the impact has been huge. Having to take that extra couple of steps to access my money has made it much easier for me to stick to the spending plan I'd set.

I've also helped a bunch of people set up this same model, and their results have been just as good. As I mentioned earlier, my clients' savings stats show that they're saving more than seven times the national average. This number sounds good, but it's even more surprising when you look at where they've come from.

Often when I start working with people, they're not saving much at all. The impact of saving at this higher rate is significant: again, as I mentioned earlier, for the average 30-year-old, it means an extra $3.4m by age 60.

Another tip is to avoid spending money from accounts with high balances, or on credit. If you have several thousand dollars in your account or use a credit card, you don't have to think about your spending. As a result, you spend more.

Instead, set up your banking to force yourself to keep track of what you spend and stop yourself from underestimating what you've spent. You'll be much clearer on how much is really left over, so you'll make fewer unnecessary purchases.

In other words, you need to reduce your potential for giving in to mindless spending, and suffering as a result. We'll dive deep into this in Chapter 4, where I'll show you how to set your money management up in a way that removes temptation.

Basically, you'll make it harder to make mistakes.

A word of warning: when you do this, you won't be choosing the thing that will give you the most pleasure IN THAT MOMENT. It probably won't feel great. But it *will* mean you're choosing the things that bring you the most pleasure overall.

Decision fatigue (willpower depletion)

The average adult makes around 35 000 decisions each day. That's a big number. You have to decide what to wear, eat and say. You have to choose how you'll act or react in different situations.

What outfit do you wear today? What path do you take crossing the road? What will you have for lunch? Which emails will you answer now and which will be put off for later? Do you tell your boss what you really think of them?

The choices we have to make just keep piling up, and most of us choose without thinking. Well, not every choice...but we do make a bunch of choices almost automatically throughout the day.

'Decision fatigue' is the concept that as you make more and more decisions throughout the day, the quality of those decisions reduces. Early in the day, before you've been overloaded with the thousands of choices you have to make, your ability to think through complex problems and find quality solutions is at its highest. There's a stack of research on this effect.

As you make more and more decisions throughout the day, the quality of those decisions reduces.

Barack Obama understands this. So does Facebook founder Mark Zuckerberg. Through his presidency, Obama only wore blue or grey suits. And while Zuckerberg has slightly different fashion sense, he still only wears one style of grey t-shirt. Yet Obama had the full resources of the United States of America, and Zuckerberg is worth over US$50 billion.

Why would two people with almost unlimited resources choose to limit their fashion choices in these ways?

Obama told Vanity Fair in an interview, 'You'll see I wear only grey or blue suits. I'm trying to pare down decisions. I don't want to make decisions about what I'm eating or wearing because I have too many other decisions to make.' Similarly, Zuckerberg says that clothing, along with breakfast, is a 'silly' decision that he doesn't want to waste time or mental energy making.

Making decision after decision is exhausting. I think everyone's been in the situation where they're working on a big project or complex task, or trying to solve a difficult problem, and had that feeling of overload. I know I've been there. By the end of the day, I'm fried and find it hard to think through even simple problems. So limiting the number of decisions to make would be worthwhile even if it's just to reduce stress.

But there's something much bigger at play.

Roy Baumeister is the founder of decision-making theory, and has done much research on decision-making behaviour. He was one of the first to examine how we use our willpower in our everyday life, and the concept of willpower as a resource. His findings changed the game for social psychology.

In his book *Willpower: Rediscovering the greatest human strength*, Baumeister mentions a study he did that involved giving participants an unsolvable problem to test their focus and self control. He wanted to examine their willpower by studying how long they'd continue to work on the problem after flexing their decision-making abilities and willpower in another area.

He first separated participants into two groups, and placed both in a waiting room before the study began. The study took place around lunchtime, and participants were told not to eat beforehand, so they came in hungry. The waiting room smelled like freshly baked cookies, and contained a table with a huge array of delicious looking sweets, chocolates, cupcakes with special sprinkles and melt-in-your-mouth chocolate chip cookies.

Baumeister cheekily ensured that all participants were tempted; but told one group that they could indulge, while giving the other radishes and telling them not to touch the sweets.

All of the participants in Baumeister's study had their work cut out for them (poor buggers): their problem was unsolvable. But the second group felt it from two directions at once. They were hungry and had to flex their willpower muscles to resist the amazing sweets, AND they had to work on this impossible problem.

So do you think that having to use willpower to avoid the sweets affected participants' decision-making?

Well, the group that could eat the sweets and didn't have to use their willpower did work on the problem for a while before eventually giving up (which was the right choice, given that it was impossible). However, the group that had to resist the temptation gave up on the problem in less than *half* the time of the first group.

Baumeister's research suggested that everyone receives a limited number of 'willpower credits' each day. Once you've used up those willpower credits, you're much more likely to give in to temptation and make choices you'll regret (either immediately or later on).

> **Everyone receives a limited number of 'willpower credits' each day.**

Have you ever been in the situation where you're doing really well in one particular area, but struggle to control yourself in others? Maybe you're working your butt off in your career, on a massive health kick that has you exercising like a beast, or eating healthily to shed some unwanted kilos. You're stoked with your progress, and everything's going well ... until you're faced with a tempting choice.

Maybe you're deciding whether to splurge on excessive amounts of junk food when your eating plan has you drinking a kale smoothie. Maybe you want to park yourself on the couch and chain-watch the entire back catalogue of The Bachelor instead of exercising. Or maybe you're thinking of splashing out on an epic trip when you know you should be saving for your first home or next investment.

Regardless of the situation, you *know* which choice you should make. You know you should eat healthy. You know you should exercise. You know you should spend less and save more. But in that moment, temptation becomes too much to bear and you give in.

You do this because you've been using so much willpower in other areas that your willpower credits are running low. You think about the decision, and deep down you know it's not the best thing to do. But in that moment, you tap out. You silence your well-behaved inner human, and you just *act*. You make a choice that brings you instant pleasure, but one you'll probably either regret or think you should have done differently later.

I've done this myself in the past. It's normally involved booking a spur-of-the-moment weekend away or holiday after a period of intense work. I've justified that holiday to myself in different ways. Sometimes I say that I've earned it through all the hard work I've put in. Or I tell myself that a win in some other area justifies the spend. Sometimes, I even say that this break or activity will help me do better in other areas of life ... and all these things are probably partly true.

But the simple fact is, if I'd made the choice with a clear mind and full willpower credits, I'd probably have chosen differently.

The concept of willpower as a limited resource has implications for how you manage (or should manage) your finances to get the money results you want. Baumeister's findings suggest that when you're forced to 'use' willpower (e.g. not spending all the money in your bank accounts), you'll tend to do worse in other willpower-dependent activities. Or, on the flip side, when you're doing great with a bunch of things in other areas (e.g. work, health, etc.), you're more likely to blow out with your money management.

Money management is a funny thing. You know what you really want. And you know what you need to do. But for some reason, you don't do it. When it comes to the crunch, you struggle to make the decisions that will get you the results you want.

For a long time, I thought this was because of a lack of motivation or resources, or some other tendency of human nature to self-sabotage. Again, I now know better.

Our inbuilt decision-making processes push us toward failure, so if you don't know how to set your finances up right, the odds are stacked against you from the start. To give your money management the best chance of success, you need to hack your decision-making processes to eliminate the impact of willpower depletion.

It's common to spend a lot of time thinking about money — not in a 'Scrooge McDuck' imagining-all-your-millions way, but instead just the day-to-day stuff. Many of the people I've helped have started from this point.

When we first started working together, these people were often so consumed that they checked their bank balances regularly throughout the day, even when nothing had changed. They spent time shuffling money around their different accounts or researching options for their money.

Once we went through the process of setting up a good strategy and a system to back it up, however, they freed up all that energy to focus on other areas. And I've noticed many of them starting to excel in other areas: in their careers, passion projects and health goals. I initially thought this was a coincidence, but the more I see it happening, the more I think it's just Baumeister's findings ringing true.

So what can you do?

Having an automated system that moves your money where it needs to go when it needs to go there has two big benefits. Firstly, it reduces the number of decisions you need to make. And secondly, it combats the effect of willpower depletion and reduces your chances of giving in to temptation.

By setting up a good money management system and structure, you're choosing the outcomes you want ahead of time. By setting up a good money management system and structure, you're choosing the outcomes you want ahead of time. Then the *real* power kicks in when you automate your strategy, because it effectively sets your defaults.

Giving that system the time and attention it deserves means setting your defaults to success, so that unless you actively 'do' something differently, you'll get your planned outcomes. After doing your initial setup, you no longer need to do anything at all to get the results you really want. There are no decisions. No test of willpower. And no temptation.

It sounds almost too good to be true.

But I assure you, it's not. I've seen this simple hack create results time and time again. It's helped a bunch of people who struggled to get the money management results they wanted for years. They never struggled with planning or figuring out what they wanted to happen. They had clear targets, budget planners, spending trackers, money management apps and tools. They were highly motivated, but they couldn't get the most important thing right. They couldn't get the outcomes they wanted.

Once they implemented this hack, though, they turned their situation around.

A solid money management structure combats many of the decision-making biases outlined in this chapter. It will help you to avoid some of the biggest roadblocks that can get between you and the financial success you want and deserve.

Don't underestimate the power of hacking your decision-making.

PUTTING IT ALL TOGETHER

We all have inherent psychological biases that impact our behaviour, so we need to keep these in check to get the results we want from our money.

Being time-poor, having to resist temptation, a tendency to stick to defaults, and decision fatigue are all interrelated; and they all impact your success with money. The good news is that you can avoid problems in all of these areas by structuring your money the right way.

Understanding the importance and impact of your many decision-making processes is the first big step toward money success. The second is building a rock-solid money management system that avoids these biases and further increases your chances of success.

Structure your money to save you time, limit temptation, set your default to success, and minimise the number of decisions you need to make and the amount of willpower you need to use. This will give a huge boost to your results and success in other areas. Automate your finances and you'll free up your time, reduce temptation, and conserve decision-making energy and willpower for other areas in life.

You'll also give yourself a giant advantage when it comes to getting the results you want.

CHAPTER 2

It pays to tame your brain

I said in Chapter 1 that the more research and work I do around money, the more I realise we're hard-wired to be unsuccessful. Basic inbuilt drivers set us up for failure, pushing us to make bad money choices and making it hard to take the actions we need to get the things we want.

This pull toward short-term satisfaction can directly conflict with your goal of getting ahead. The desire to live life to the fullest, travel and jam-pack as many experiences as possible into the time you have leads to slower progress toward the money success and future you want.

The way that you manage money today is also driven by technology, credit and personal finance companies with very smart product manufacturers. This makes achieving real money success more challenging than ever before because these companies have teams of people working to make it easier than ever for you to spend more money.

Another way you're influenced is by comparing yourself to people in your social media circles, peer groups, and personal and professional networks. You see Instagram stories of your mates' epic vacays around Europe.

Or perhaps they're splurging on the hottest new restaurants, or buying new tech toys and luxury gear. Then you start wanting that stuff yourself, and want to live that life.

We all have an inbuilt desire to 'keep up' with the people around us. This can make you afraid to make dumb decisions that could result in being left behind or make you look like a fool. It's natural to want every decision you make to be a good one.

We also don't want to do anything we'll regret later. This can push you into a never-ending (and impossible) quest to find the best possible choices. It can also delay you in taking the actions you need to get the results you want.

Then there's the fact that the odds really are against us. So, based on your inbuilt psychological drivers, you're pretty much destined for failure from birth. You actually have very little hope of doing what's needed to get ahead.

Combine *this* with the financial overconfidence that our 'you can do anything' culture breeds, which can lead you to ignore risks you should carefully consider. Then, add our digitally-enabled age of information overload...and you've got a potent mix that makes failure more common than success.

But all is not lost. There is hope. You *can* prevail. I told you in Chapter 1 that you can 'hack' your thinking to make getting what you want easier. But to do this, you need to know the rules of the game. You need to know the money psychology basics and understand their impact. And you need to know how to recognise when your thinking is sabotaging you.

Urgent vs important

In Chapter 1, I told you that we humans have an inbuilt tendency to procrastinate by focusing on seemingly urgent things. After all, there are *plenty* of them. There's that work crisis you get dragged into. You need to constantly check emails through the day. Then there's that seven-part miniseries on Netflix about the guy who does the thing and then other things happen but then the twist comes and OH MY GOD YOU JUST CAN'T MISS IT…

These 'urgent' activities have a nasty habit of stealing your attention, and it's never been easier to fill your days with them.

I also introduced you to the many things in life that are important but not urgent. Getting fit and healthy. Extending your professional development to take your career to the next level. Building quality relationships with the people who are important to you. Getting your money sorted.

These things are never really 'urgent' until they reach crisis point, and the crises can take different forms. Your health actually starts to suffer. You end up stuck in a company you don't like, in a role you hate, under a boss you despise. Your partner becomes unhappy, or other important relationships break down. You get close to wanting to wind back from work and the daily grind and realise you don't have enough money to fund the lifestyle you want to live.

Once the problem becomes urgent, you need to take immediate action. But if you've let it get to this point, your chances of being able to fix it are much lower. At the very least, it'll take extra hard work and pain to make it happen. So why do we neglect the things that are really important for our long-term happiness?

Like I said above, it's because we're procrastinators. This isn't a new idea: it's something that's intrigued people for many years. Former U.S. President Dwight Eisenhower first pushed the 'urgent vs important' principle into the public eye in a speech in 1954. Shortly afterward, it was nicknamed 'The Eisenhower Principle'.

Steven Covey also wrote about this principle in *The Seven Habits of Highly Effective People*, an epic book that many super-successful people cite as one of their most formative reads. And time and time again, these people have said that much of their success is built around their ability to focus on what's important and ignore any distractions.

The 'urgent vs important' principle can be broken down into the matrix outlined below. Every activity you undertake every single day can be classified into one of four categories.

The urgent vs important matrix

Activity Type	Urgent	Not Urgent
Important	Urgent and Important	Important and Not Urgent
Not Important	Urgent and Not Important	Not Important and Not Urgent

I've broken down what these sections mean below.

Urgent and important

These are problems or situations that require your immediate attention and lead to an immediate outcome, often requiring you to work at full capacity to reach a tight deadline. You expend a lot of energy in this zone though, so consistently working here isn't sustainable and can lead to burnout.

Unfortunately, these types of activities pop up more often than we'd like them to, so it's easy to fall into the trap of working entirely in this space. And of course, many people end up here through procrastination. Neglecting things that start out as 'important and not urgent' means they end up *becoming* urgent as the deadline gets closer.

If, on the other hand, you allocate time to these activities, you'll stop them from becoming urgent.

Urgent and not important

These activities often result from other people's requests. They can seem urgent because the person who's asking for your help places importance on them. And in the heat of the moment, it's easy to assume that they're also 'important to you'.

Regularly doing this can get you stuck in this space, however—and that won't get you any closer to YOUR personal goals. Sometimes you need to politely say 'No' and decline to get dragged into other people's crises.

Important and not urgent

These activities are the ones that can help you achieve important personal goals. But if you don't make time for them, it's easy to fill the space with other tasks and be busy without being effective.

Of course, making time is tricky. We've all been there. You get thinking about a task or project that can help you get something you really want. You get all pumped up about the ultimate result you'll get from doing it. You're ready to go—either you put time aside for it, or just jump right in and get cracking straight away.

But then your phone goes off, you get a flood of emails, or someone pulls you into a conversation. The going gets difficult, you lose motivation and your important goals are suddenly on the back burner.

To see these activities through, you need to avoid the distractions. That's hard, but the results are worth it.

Not important and not urgent

These are distractions or things other people want you to do that don't achieve anything of value for you. They can also include wasting time on social media or other activities that don't move you any closer to your personal goals.

These distractions add no value to your life apart from giving you some downtime. Yes, *some* downtime is a must, but if you spend too much time in this space thinking you're doing something important, you'll never really achieve anything.

So try to cut these activities out wherever possible.

How to make this work for you

Because the 'important but not urgent' tasks bring you closer to your personal goals, there's an argument for spending all (or at least most) of your time here. The people who 'win' at life generally build good habits around allocating solid amounts of time to these tasks. Unlike most people, they prioritise activities such as their health and fitness, personal relationships, career and professional development, and money.

I've said before that making smart money choices and ensuring your money success falls squarely into the 'important but not urgent' column. You *know* it's important to have money and be secure. You want the lifestyle benefits of financial independence.

But, if you're like most people, you get distracted. You struggle to focus. You get tempted by short-term expenses like that impromptu dinner out because you're too lazy to cook, the big night out with mates, or that new tech toy that'll change your life so much for the better that YOU'VE JUST GOTTA HAVE IT.

This spending can seem important and/or urgent in the moment, but it doesn't bring any lasting value. If you prioritise spending on these things, you can't use that money for bigger, more rewarding future expenses (i.e. the *actual* important spending).

Procrastination in practice

My first financial advice job was for a traditional suit-and-tie company that specialised in helping people at the end of their careers to set up their money to provide for their retirement. Our clients were typically aged 50+, and had usually built up a solid amount of money over the years. But they weren't all that way.

Some people who came to us were in the same age bracket and also wanted to retire in the next 5-10 years. Their financial situation looked quite different though. They were in a mess: they knew they wanted to finish work soon, but couldn't see how that could happen. This was always a sad thing to see, but one of these clients in particular has stuck with me.

I was introduced to a lovely lady in her early 50s who I'll call Angela. Angela was an executive who'd made a very healthy income, but had little to show for it. She loved travelling and enjoying her lifestyle, and she'd done a good job of it.

I always love to talk travel, and Angela had plenty of great travel stories. She also lived a very comfortable lifestyle when she wasn't travelling: enjoying nice restaurants, good wine and catching up with family and friends. In fact, Angela had enjoyed her lifestyle so much that, for most of her working career, she'd spent almost all her income on 'urgent today' expenses, without allocating much to the 'important tomorrow'.

That meant Angela and I needed to have some tough conversations. Because she'd left it so late, it was impossible for her to retire on the income she was used to, not even by drastically cutting back her day-to-day spending (which she did NOT want to do).

She wanted to retire at age 60, but that was out of the question. Even if she worked to age 70 and saved most of what she earned, she still wouldn't get close to a retirement income she was comfortable with.

Angela wasn't happy with any of the options available to her. She didn't want to work to 70. She didn't want to retire on $30k p.a. Nor did she want to cut back her lifestyle drastically and save all her income. But sadly, those were the only options on the table for her.

Angela's story doesn't have a happy ending. But will yours?

Like with most things, the longer you wait to get your money sorted, the more difficult it becomes to get what you want. There are only so many 'levers' you can pull to get more money. And when time isn't on your side, your options decrease even further. If you wait too long, you could be forced to make tough choices just like Angela was. You'll have to save more, spend less, run more risk in your investment strategy, or settle for less in the future.

And I think ALL of these are bad results.

Angela had neglected the 'important but not urgent' activity of getting her money sorted for so long that she'd eliminated her options. She wasn't alone in this, and the frustrating thing for me was that she could have avoided it all.

Angela had been making good money for 30 years. By regularly saving just a small amount over that time and investing the money, Angela could have retired at the age she wanted, on the income she wanted, and had the lifestyle she wanted along the way.

This is the case with all other 'important but not urgent' activities. If you wait until you have a health crisis, it's much harder to get back into shape. If you let your relationships break down, it's harder to get them back. If you stop pushing yourself forward at work, you end up pigeonholed into a role you hate.

> **If you let important things become urgent, you'll struggle to fix them and get them back to the point they were at before you let them slip.**

If you let important things become urgent, you'll struggle to fix them and get them back to the point they were at before you let them slip.

Make the important things happen

The first thing you need to do is make a choice. You can't have one foot in and one foot out: you need to consciously prioritise your important tasks. I'm just talking about money here, but if you apply this process to all the other important areas of your life I mentioned above, you'll notice huge benefits. You have to work at things you know are important, focusing on longer-term benefits and accepting that there won't be an immediate payoff.

Next, you need to avoid distractions. Block out some dedicated time in your diary to work on your money management. During this time, flick your phone to 'Do Not Disturb' and log out of your socials. Give your money solid, uninterrupted time so you can actually make progress.

Then, break whatever you need to do down into small steps. Getting the best results from your money involves many different moving parts, which can seem overwhelming. Breaking down the overall task into the bite-sized chunks will help you to make steady progress, and give you that all-important momentum and motivation because you know you're moving towards the end result you want.

Another thing that can help keep you moving forward is having an accountability partner. This is someone to keep you accountable for the targets you've set or outcomes you want. Ideally, use someone who's good with money and understands the results you're going after. Even better, use someone who has successfully done what you want to do themselves (or who's done it for someone else, like a good financial adviser).

The sooner you commit to being successful with money and taking action to make it happen, the smaller the adjustments you'll need to make. That means the easier it will be to get what you want. You'll have to sacrifice less, and you'll create more options for yourself.

So please, get started. NOW. Make it happen.

I'm clearly a little biased, given what I do, but I don't think much in life is more important than making sure you're successful with money. This will help you look after the people you love. It will help you live the lifestyle you want. It will mean you never have to suck up to a crappy boss and be stuck in a soul-crushing job you hate.

The sooner you commit to being successful with money and taking action to make it happen, the smaller the adjustments you'll need to make.

So dedicate the time and energy to focusing on your personal money goals—the things that aren't urgent now, but will bring you huge benefits in the future.

Do this and you'll get the things YOU really want.

Settle for 'good' now rather than 'the best' in the distant future

I'm not a fan of having to 'settle'. Ever. The word actually makes me cringe: I want the things I want, and I don't want to settle for less.

> **When it comes to investing, though, sometimes settling is the best thing you can do.**

When it comes to investing, though, sometimes settling is the best thing you can do.

I spoke at a recent Sydney event about money management and investing; and in the Q&A session that followed, a well-dressed guy in his early 30s jumped in with a question. He wanted to invest in property, and had done a lot of research to figure out the very best suburb for his investment.

He mentioned that he was good with numbers (an engineer), and that he'd built spreadsheets to analyse rental income on properties in different suburbs and compare it to the growth in property values in those same suburbs. He described the countless hours he'd spent analysing trends to find that perfect investment that would make him big money.

Obviously frustrated, he told me that after researching for over 12 months, he still felt no closer to finding the best suburb. Instead, he just felt super-confused.

It's completely normal to think you need to find the absolute best option whenever you make a choice. You want the best career, the best partner, the best place to live, and the best place to take a holiday. Your psychology pushes you to go for the best, and to never settle.

But is this another case of psychology working against you?

Our engineer friend had clearly gone a little over the top with his research, but the situation is more common than you might think. It's IMPOSSIBLE to know which suburbs will be the best to invest in. There are investment companies with significant resources that would love to know the best place to buy property, and would make a lot of money if they did.

I'll let you in on a secret though: nobody has cracked that code.

I don't want to get into a detailed discussion of investment theory here, but let's just say that investment markets are driven by investors. Those investors are people, and people can be irrational. This means it's impossible to say which investment will perform best over ANY time period. It also means that even a 'sure thing' isn't, because people don't always do what we expect.

So I don't know which suburb would be the best possible investment. What I do know is that whether you'd invested in Bondi, Darlinghurst or Pyrmont in Sydney, or New Farm, Ascot or Teneriffe in Queensland (or any other super-central suburbs close to fast growing capital cities), the amount of money you'd have made on your investment wouldn't have been hugely different.

Everyone knows that these suburbs are all solid investments, but when you start to take action, you lose sight of this. You get caught up trying to somehow divine which one will be 'best' and make the most money.

I've met many people who've spent countless hours on investment research. This is nothing more than wasted time. Actually, it's worse than wasted time: the delay stops them taking action and investing their money. And taking the action is the most valuable thing you can do.

> **Settling for 'good' and taking action now will always give you a better result than waiting for the 'best' investment years into the future.**

Settling for 'good' and taking action now will always give you a better result than waiting for the 'best' investment years into the future. In most cases, that future investment won't even happen. So don't get caught up in the spin when you invest. Don't believe that there's some secret formula you can follow to find the next 'hotspot'.

All the so-called gurus would have you think they know all the secrets. Trust me, they don't. If they did, they'd just invest all their own money and keep the millions for themselves. Anyone who tells you otherwise has an agenda that's probably more focused on them than on you.

Now, don't get me wrong. You want your investments to be good—that's super-important. I'm not saying to pick stocks by throwing darts at the newspaper, invest in your neighbour's next big startup idea, or flush your money down the toilet. You want anything you invest in to perform well and make you money.

But what you can't do is find the very best option before investing. Nobody ever knows what that option is until after the data is in, and by then it's too late. So don't waste time and delay taking action. Don't let your psychology make you think you need to make the absolute-best-possible-cannot-be-beaten choice of *all* time. That will just stop you from taking action.

Find an investment that's going to be good, and just go for it. Now. Put your money in. Then let time and the magic of compound interest do its thing. Set your money to work. Don't leave it on the sidelines—all you'll do is miss the opportunity for a great result in the hopeless quest to get the best one.

I can't believe I'm about to say this, but in this one, single, solitary, exception-less case, you should settle.

Overconfidence

We humans are a confident bunch. And confidence is important. We're told to believe in ourselves. We're told about the benefits of positive thinking. Our parents tell us anything is possible. 'Confidence is king,' they say. 'Think positive,' they say. 'Believe in yourself. You can do anything.'

So over your life, it's easy to build your confidence to the point you do actually believe you can do almost anything. But your confidence around money can end up being much higher than it should be. This can make you ignore risks that you should carefully consider, and play up the chances of a particular investment or strategy being a success.

There's much research that shows how your confidence levels impact the choices you make. Daniel Kahneman is a Nobel Prize winning economist who spent much of his career researching the factors that impact our choices. In his book *Thinking Fast and Slow*, he found that when you really want a particular outcome or result, you're more likely to incorrectly assess the risk involved or the probability of that result falling through.

When you really want a particular outcome or result, you're more likely to incorrectly assess the risk involved or the probability of that result falling through.

You've probably experienced this watching your favourite sports team. You might be watching with a friend who supports the other team, and you're both confident that *your* team will win. You both really want your own team to win, so in your minds, you play up their chance of success and downplay their risk of failing. Sometimes the odds are definitively stacked against them, but you still think they're in with a reasonable chance.

I know I've experienced this as a fan of the Wallabies (the Australian Rugby Union team) in recent years. If you know rugby, you'll know that the Wallabies just aren't performing right now. Yet every game, I still give them a reasonable chance. I think, *'If they just get these few things right, they're in with a shot'* ...but sadly, they continue to disappoint.

And the funny thing is that when the next game comes around, I still feel the same way. Kahneman's findings ring true here. Because I really WANT this outcome (for the Wallabies to win), I overconfidently assess their chances of success.

Now imagine you have some money you want to invest. You do your research. You talk to a few people. You might even get professional advice. Then it happens: you find an investment opportunity in a company.

You hear stories about its high chances of success. You do more research, and find a couple of articles supporting your view. You think about the potential. This company could be the next big thing in its space. It could rival the big players. You could make a bunch of money. You weigh up your decision.

Now let me ask you: how much do you want this outcome?

Chances are that you want to be the sort of person who finds good investments and makes smart choices. You also want your investment to make you a bunch of money so you can cruise around the Mediterranean like a rock star, snapping off a chain series of Insta-stories that highlight your epic-ness and go viral. You want to end up on Oprah, talking about how you always believed in yourself and never quit and that's why it all happened and anyone else can do it too, if they just BELIEVE IN THEMSELVES...

So what do you think this desire does to your chance of objectively assessing the opportunity?

Kahneman's research shows that your natural bias towards overconfidence *will* negatively impact your assessment. You'll ignore many of the risks involved. You'll instinctively overstate the positive attributes of the investment. And you'll overlook issues that you'd pay attention to in any other situation.

Money is an emotional topic. It's almost impossible *not* to get emotional about making, losing and spending it. This response is baked into our DNA, which makes it difficult to make the objective assessment you need to make smart investment choices.

Then, as a further complication, another inbuilt human bias is the belief that our own involvement will somehow impact the outcome. In his book, Kahneman mentions another group of behavioural finance researchers who discovered this bias through their studies. Stephen Ferris, Robert Haugen, and Anil Makhija found that people are likely to bet more on a coin toss if the coin has yet to be tossed. By contrast, if the coin had already been tossed but the outcome of the toss had been concealed, people would bet a lower amount on the result.

Let's slow that down. This study found that if a coin has already been tossed and we don't know the outcome, we think we're less likely to correctly guess the outcome. We think that just BEING PRESENT during the toss gives us a better chance of correctly choosing the result. Does that make sense to you? This is our beautifully human overconfidence at its very best.

This effect is called the 'involvement bias', and it contributes to our overconfidence.

For regular investing (e.g. buying shares in a company, investing in property, or choosing super fund investment options), your involvement or participation will have ABSOLUTELY no impact on the investment's chances of success. You're simply a passenger. But the involvement bias makes you think otherwise. You believe that getting involved makes your investment more likely to be successful. This flawed thinking has led many people to make poor investment choices.

Our biases are built in and can't be turned off, but we can minimise and manage their impact. To counter biases, you need to hack your thinking and choose investments that avoid their impact. I'll cover this in detail in Section 3.

The illusion of knowledge

There's one more psychological bias you should understand to get better results from your money. It's natural to think that more information can only help you make better decisions. It doesn't seem to make sense that you'd make worse choices with more information. But, of course, you're human.

In his book *The Psychology of Investing*, John Nofsinger talks about predicting the roll of a fair, six-sided dice. If you roll a fair dice, the probability of any given number coming up is an even one-in-six chance. So if someone's about to roll a dice and they ask you to predict the outcome, each of the six numbers has *exactly* the same chance of being rolled. And we typically know this when we're asked this question in isolation.

But if we're equipped with additional information, something interesting happens.

If you're told that a dice has been rolled five times and that all five rolls turned up a four, psychology kicks in. Some people think another four is more likely to come up, while others think it's less likely. The key is that they think knowing what's happened in the past will help them predict what will happen in the future. They think that previous results have an impact on the probability of the next result.

In reality, of course, the probability is unchanged. There's still a one-in-six chance of any given number coming up when the dice is rolled. This is a classic example of how more information can lead us to make a worse decision.

This bias also impacts money management and investment choices. You might hear about the performance of a stock investment or a property region or area, and think this past performance will impact the future performance. In fact, the probability of any particular result is unchanged. Many people have fallen for this trap, thinking that an investment's poor performance in the past is an anomaly, and that its fortunes should turn around at any minute. So they invest and often pay the price.

In my work as a Financial Adviser, I've unfortunately come across many people who've lost considerable money as a result of following this investment 'strategy'. They've tried to pick investments that have underperformed, waiting for the quick bounce back and resulting profit. But when an investment or company underperforms, there's typically a good reason. Investing in that company doesn't mean its performance will magically turn around.

If only it were that easy.

PUTTING IT ALL TOGETHER

It turns out that we humans are wired for failure, at least in money terms. We focus on non-important-but-urgent activities, never want to settle for less than the best, are overconfident about our chances of success, and think the information we read online about the investment we're considering puts us in a better position to invest.

Weighing up options, overconfidence, endless research and distraction all usually sidetrack us well before we take any action at all. These biases are subtle and can often go unnoticed, but their impact is significant, and can seem to doom us to failure.

Combating these biases and decision-making flaws is no easy feat. You need to firstly understand them, and then keep them in mind when you make your money decisions. It's not easy, but it is possible.

(continued)

To counteract them, you need to hack your thinking. Maintaining your focus and objectivity is critical for money success. And you can't avoid these biases in isolation, either: you need to consider them all together as part of your complete money strategy.

But there is hope. You can prevail. Follow the proven process in this book, and you'll be well on your way to cutting through the noise and getting the results you deserve from your money.

CHAPTER 3

Why you don't have a six-pack

It's common to want to do better financially. But if you're new to 'adulting' with money, it can be pretty confusing and even overwhelming—even if you're initially excited about taking action.

I see this often when running money education events. People read a few blogs, speak to some of their mates and maybe their family, or they might even read a book or two. Then they chat to me, all pumped up to do something to drive better results. In that moment, they're as excited as a 15-year-old girl about to attend her first Bieber concert. I can almost physically feel the enthusiasm.

But they don't always get the results they want. When I speak to the same people months later, the enthusiastic 15-year-old pop princess has transformed into a 17-year-old goth. The enthusiasm has morphed into a mixture of regret, frustration and self-loathing.

This happens for a few reasons, and through this chapter I'll help you understand them so you know how to avoid the same torment happening to you.

First though, let's take an example: a recent workshop I ran where I got to chatting with a young couple. They wanted to buy their first home, and had a bunch of questions during the session. Then they stayed at the end to fire a stack more at me. The guy in particular was super-detail-focused, so I answered in more depth than I normally would. I suggested a few topics and sources for research, and they seemed like the DIY sort of people who want to go it alone so I sent them on their way.

A few weeks later, they reached back out and told me they felt more confused and further away from making a decision than when they'd first started. I spent some time chatting to them about why they felt this way. It took me a while to get it out of them, but in the end, they confessed they were afraid. They were pretty sure they had the right strategy. They'd lined everything up as best they could. But they just weren't ready to pull the trigger.

They worried that deep down, they'd missed something that would cause them problems either now or in the future. They also felt ashamed of their fear—as though they should be able to figure it out and conquer it all on their own.

We ended up working together to build out a plan that covered all the bases (as we'll discuss in Section 2). At the end of this process, their confidence levels were through the roof and they were finally ready to take action.

Over time, I've spoken to a lot of people about their money. And I think it's fair to say that most people's personal finances are a bit of a mess. Occasionally, I meet someone who's really on top of things: not necessarily filthy rich, but just getting good results from their finances. They might be saving well, investing, paying down debt or something else. Whatever it is, they're clear on what they're doing, and are getting some wins from their money.

When this happens, I always ask them how they got to where they are now. I love knowing how things work, and—as I've mentioned before—I enjoy a good hack, so I've spent time understanding what makes the difference between money mediocrity and success.

On top of this, I regularly review my advice and coaching services to understand which elements get the results for my clients. And when I do this and speak to successful people, the same thing keeps coming up.

The people who get positive results are taking action. It's that simple.

Or is it?

The people who get positive results are taking action. It's that simple.

Fear is natural. It's what stops us from doing dangerous things. You'd be stupid to walk along the very edge of a tall building, jump out of a moving car, or tell your boss what you really think of some of their decisions.

And when you're first starting to build up your savings and investments, it's important to be cautious. The first $50k you save or grow through investing will be the hardest and slowest $50k you ever make. And once you've reached this point, you don't want to do something dumb that loses you a bunch of money and pushes you back to the starting line.

So you want to do your research and understand your options. And all power to you. You live in the information age, where everything you could ever want or need to know is available online. Your smartphone brings all this information right to your couch, bus stop or even bathroom.

But, as we discussed in Chapter 2, more information *doesn't* lead to better decisions. In fact, I read an interesting quote the other day from Derek Sivers—a successful entrepreneur and one of the pioneers of digital music—in Tim Ferris's book *Tools of Titans*:

If information was the answer, we'd all be billionaires with perfect abs.

This quote jumped out at me because I've seen its impact time and time again. I've seen people who've done loads of research online, attended a workshop, or had it all laid out for them into an overall plan. They've had everything they needed to act.

But they didn't.

Early on in my career, I got so frustrated watching this happen that I just wanted to shake people and say, 'You know what you need to do. NOW YOU JUST HAVE TO DO IT.'

I now know that, like Sivers said in the quote above, more information does not get you results. It's actually the opposite: a bunch of research has proven that more information slows down your decision-making process.

This research has been carried out by ultra-legit sources like PhD professors from the world's leading universities and research centres, the Harvard Business Review, and Huffington Post, among countless others. And I've seen this effect myself many times in practice.

Given the topic in question, I don't suggest diving into the research. Instead, here's the Blinkist version in a sentence: the studies all found that the more information you consume, the LESS likely you are to be able to make any choice at all.

In his book The Paradox of Choice, Barry Schwartz talked about a study that found unless you act on your research immediately, you'll lose over 75 per cent of the information you've 'learnt'. It's no wonder that when I connect with someone at the first stage of their research journey and then catch up with them months later, they're feeling frustrated.

In the same book, Schwartz did a study on retirement funds in the US. This study found that when a fund member had a small number of investment options available, they were highly likely to make a choice. But for every additional investment option added, the fund member was a few percent less likely to make any choice at all. I've come up with a highly mathematical formula to explain this concept below:

More options ➔ more confusion ➔ less likely to make a choice

When it comes to money options this problem is even worse, because there are so many mixed messages and so much conflicting information. If you've ever looked into making an investment or taking other actions with your money, you've already experienced this. You get completely different viewpoints from different people, and way more ideas or opinions than you really want or need.

Your parents tell you to buy a property in the 'burbs' and throw everything into the mortgage.

Your bestie tells you that you should buy an investment property in Tasmania.

Your boss tells you to buy some tricky stock options on European banks (because they're GOING places, of course).

Your personal trainer tells you about how he's made a bunch of money buying carpark spaces and renting them out.

Your Uber driver tells you to buy shares in North Queensland almond plantations...

Each person passionately *swears* by their suggestion and insists that they're right and everyone else is wrong. And with every new option you hear, you die a little inside. Your head feels like it will explode at any minute. You just want to shake someone and scream, 'CAN'T YOU JUST AGREE!'

Of course, everyone agreeing *would* make your life easier. You could just trust the consensus and jump in. But it's not that easy. You don't need more information. You don't need another idea. You don't need another opinion. You need to act.

Again, I'm not saying you shouldn't do your research. You should make smart choices. But you can make it easier to avoid information overload and analysis paralysis with research-based hacks that I've seen work in practice.

Find a single source of truth

When you're making a decision, it's natural to want to get a number of different viewpoints. But for big decisions, this will work against you. Remember: the more options you have, the more confused you become. When you can see the merits of these many different options and don't know which to choose, you end up confused and doing nothing.

To put yourself in a position to take action, you need to find a single, solid resource you can rely on. You need ONE person, company or institution that will give you good information, advice, guidance and motivation. And most importantly, this resource needs to make you feel confident that you're making the right decision.

When choosing this resource, the key things to look for are:

- **A solid understanding of your available options**. If you're looking to invest, your resource needs to be across the different types of investment options, and the advantages and downsides of each. This allows them to inform you of your options, and help you understand each one's merits.

- **Knowledge of what's important to you, and how your situation and what's important may change over time**. If you aren't fully aware of these things yourself, you may end up either ignoring options that could work really well for you, or making a choice that's good for you now but not so good in the future. And if you don't know these things now, your resource needs to be able to help you figure them out by asking probing questions that get you thinking.

- **Real, positive experience with the option/s you're considering**. Your resource may have been successful with each option themselves, or seen others be successful with it firsthand. But don't take money advice from someone who's always broke. Don't take property advice from someone who's a slave to their mortgage. And don't take advice from someone who's done a bunch of research online but never actually successfully invested anything themselves.

- **Previous success with money generally**. This is an extension of the previous point that makes logical sense, but is often overlooked. People get caught up taking money advice from someone who's an authority in other areas, thinking this authority transfers. It could be your boss, your parents or dentist—someone you trust, respect and may even love. But just because they're good in a bunch of other areas, it doesn't mean they're the best person to give you advice about money.

- **An ability to push you to take action**. You need someone who can confidently tell you what you should do and why. The problem with getting advice from your mates or family is that they're often hesitant to push you when you need to be pushed. They don't want the responsibility that comes from being the guiding force behind your big decision. So you end up with a hesitant suggestion that doesn't give you the confidence you need to act.

Once you find a resource that ticks the boxes above, you don't need to spend more time researching. You don't need to delay action further or wait for the perfect time. If your resource has the experience, understanding and ability to advise and push you to act, you don't need anyone else's viewpoint.

You just need to act.

Keep it simple

The simplest strategies, investments and tools are often the best. There's no need to complicate your situation or confuse yourself with anything tricky. The only people who make money from really complex strategies or investments are the ones who sell them (or the services to get you into them) in the first place.

I've seen people 'invest' in racehorses, complex share options and derivatives, precious metals, currency, paper mills, olive groves, complex property leverage strategies, carparks, and even prize bull semen. None of those investors achieved the results they were looking for, and many of them lost a *lot* of money in the process.

> **The most common strategies are the most common for a reason: they work.**

Buying shares or property, saving money at the bank, and investing in your super are the most common (and the least sexy) strategies. But sexy isn't always best—and when it comes to money, boring can be very effective and attractive to boot. The most common strategies are the most common for a reason: they work.

Don't get caught up in the hype. The glossy brochures, the marketing messages, the buzz words, the fancy snacks at 'information sessions'...these can all distract you from the two most important things you should understand, which are the return you should realistically expect and the level of risk involved.

When you're young and have heaps of time on your side, you don't need to shoot the lights out with every investment. You just need something to give you solid, stable, steady returns over time, and *reduce your chance of loss*. Keeping it simple makes these results easier to achieve.

So why do so many people opt for complex strategies? It's because normally, the more complex your strategy is, the higher its expected returns. In isolation, this would be a good thing. But higher expected returns ALWAYS come with higher levels of risk. And if you want to reduce your chances of setbacks and momentum-killing mistakes, you want to reduce your risk as much as possible.

Keeping things simple also gives you a lot more peace of mind. That's because you'll have a good handle on your strategy, and clearly understand what you're doing. This understanding will make you more comfortable, reduce your stress levels, and give you confidence that you're headed in the right direction. Don't make things complex when you can get the results you want by keeping things simple.

Apply your common sense

While you may not be an expert in personal finance, your intuition and feelings are a good indicator of whether or not something is right for you. Whether you're buying a new pair of shoes, trying out a new gym class, or choosing toppings at your favourite fro-yo bar—if something doesn't feel right, you should pause and take stock.

Apply this same thinking to your money. If you don't fully understand and feel comfortable with a decision, it's not going to be right for you. (The only caveat for this is the need to understand your psychological biases and their impact on your decision-making.)

Even if an option you're considering is 'good' in absolute terms, it won't be good for you if you're not comfortable with it because you'll lack confidence. This may lead you to doubt your strategy, which in turn can lead to making poor choices, investing when you shouldn't, or pulling out of investments at the wrong time. A lack of confidence will also increase your stress levels and reduce your sleep-at-night factor.

So apply an overlay of common sense to your decision-making process to build true confidence.

Use a Financial Adviser or Coach

I understand this isn't right for everyone, but there are three benefits of having a Financial Adviser or Coach to help you with your money:

- They help with your research.
- They push you to take action.
- They keep you focused and accountable.

Any Financial Adviser worth their salt will be across all the key areas we talked about being necessary in a resource. They'll have already done the research on all the potentially worthwhile strategies for you. They'll work with you to uncover what's truly important now, and how this might change over time. They'll have practical experience with all the options you are (or should be) thinking about. And they'll push you to act when you need a gentle nudge.

They can do all this because they've already helped a bunch of people do it all before. They've seen what works and what doesn't. And they know the common mistakes people make, and the roadblocks that slow them down.

That means they'll be able to discuss any options you've been thinking about with you. They'll help you understand how each option applies to your situation, and uncover any potential downsides. They're also likely to be able to suggest other potentially relevant options you hadn't considered.

> **The best option for you always depends on where you're at, what you want, and how you feel about different options.**

You'll still need to choose what you're most comfortable with yourself, because no one strategy is best for everyone. The best option for you always depends on where you're at, what you want, and how you feel about different options. But a professional will be able to explain what's most important for you to think about, and then ask the key questions you need to answer to establish the best strategy for you.

So choosing to outsource in this area will save you time, give you more confidence, help you make better choices, and probably make you aware of other options you hadn't considered.

And remember the Sivers quote at the start of this chapter too: information without action is meaningless.

We've all been there. You read a book about exercise, nutrition, or personal or professional development. You get some great ideas, and feel ready to take action. But then the book gets buried under mail or tidied into a drawer. A flood of emails comes in, or you get caught up creating the best Instagram story ever seen. Regardless, you don't end up actually taking action.

Avoiding information overload is important, but it's only half the battle. You still need to ACT, which can be challenging when you're juggling all the other things in your life.

This is where it can be helpful to have an accountability loop: a mechanism for keeping you accountable for the things you said you'd do to get the things you want. In other words: someone to push you.

I must admit I'm a bit of a coaching junkie. I have a business coach, a multimedia coach, a mindfulness coach, a mentor, and a peer accountability group. I meet with these people regularly to help me get results in different areas of my personal and professional life.

You might question the value of this network. I'm a pretty motivated person. I feel that even working alone, I'd work hard and probably get decent results. Working with my coaches and accountability partners generates even better results, though. One of the biggest benefits by FAR is the accountability loop that the coaching relationship creates.

Now, don't get me wrong. These coaches know much more than me in their areas of speciality and give me great tips and insights about things I wouldn't have otherwise considered. But the accountability loop that pushes me to take action is still the biggest benefit.

I know that if I go to my business coaching session without having completed my action items, I won't make good use of the time or the money I'm spending on the session. If I see my multimedia coach without having completed the projects I was tasked with, he'll be disappointed and I won't be using my time with him effectively.

So I actually do the work (most of the time), and get better results sooner. Sometimes things do get in the way, and I don't get as far as I'd like.

Still, my session with my accountability partner gives me the gentle push and motivation I need to keep things moving.

Money is another area where accountability generates better results. The first step with money is always the hardest—whether it's getting your savings sorted, starting an investment plan, buying property or starting a business. Having someone to give you advice and guidance, narrow down your research, and push you to act will help you take that step sooner and with more confidence.

The short-term benefits of acting now are a confidence boost and reduced stress. But perhaps just as important is the long-term financial benefit of increased compounding returns. This means reaching targets sooner and/or with less sacrifice. Personally, I feel the confidence and reduced stress alone would more than cover the time and money you invest in getting help, but the extra money you make long-term will definitely offset any costs involved (and then some).

The sooner you start investing, the more you amplify your results. For example, if you'd started from $0 and had invested only $10 per day (or $3650 annually) into the Australian share market over the last 20 years, you'd have around $175k today. BUT, if you'd started 10 years sooner (total 30 years), you'd now have over $460k (extra $285k). Starting another 10 years before that (total 40 years) would make your money worth over $1.1m (extra $925k) today.

Note: The figures above are based on the average long-term return on the Australian share market (8.6 per cent). We'll dive more into this when we cover investing, but for now, note that this is a reasonable return to expect.

What sort of difference would that amount of money make for you?

This basic example shows the benefits of acting sooner. Even if you invested $100 000 in good advice to set your strategy and then push you to act, your investment would be returned many times over.

If you're struggling to take action, worried about making mistakes, or finding it hard to take a leap on an investment you'd thought about in the past, ask yourself whether you need some help. Be brutally honest here: it's just the two of us and I won't tell ☺.

Are you doing nothing because you're struggling with information overload and worried about making a mistake?

Are you avoiding taking action because you're overwhelmed with options?

Or are you maybe (just maybe) experiencing procrastination that's holding you back?

If you answered yes to any of these, seek some help.

The benefits you'll get will far outweigh the time and money you invest.

PUTTING IT ALL TOGETHER

I hate seeing people suffering through inaction. Inertia is actually my least favourite word, and my biggest pet hate. The costs are high, both in terms of missed opportunities and the stress of not being on top of your money. Information overload and analysis paralysis are real factors, and big roadblocks that will slow you down if you don't do something to avoid them.

Don't fall into the trap of information paralysis. It can threaten your ability to act, but you can successfully navigate it. You can always tweak, refine and adjust your strategy later, so the direction you take now doesn't have to be the path you follow forever.

Just like with an ocean liner, getting started is always the most difficult part. It's much easier to course-correct once you're moving, so don't delay. Avoid the inertia trap that's so common when it comes to money, and get started on the path to the results you want. TODAY.

Follow the steps above and you'll be all set to push through inaction and start getting the results you want. Find a good resource, make them your
(continued)

single source of truth, and stop the constant quest for more options. Don't complicate your strategy more than you need to—keeping it simple will make you feel more confident in what you're doing. Use the common sense test to avoid the hype vortex that sucks so many people into crazy strategies and investments. And finally get yourself an accountability partner to push you forward if you need it.

Taking action now will pay big dividends. You'll feel better about what you're doing with money, and have more confidence and less stress. You'll also make more money over time, and reach your targets sooner.

CHAPTER 4

Why you suck at saving

At any stage in life, how much you spend and save has a huge impact on your money results. But in your 20s, 30s and 40s, they're the *biggest* drivers of those results. They drive whether you should invest at all, how much you should invest, what sort of investments you should use, and how you manage your money every single day.

And if you don't have a good strategy in place and a good system to support it, making any progress at all will be tough.

The last three chapters have been a little heavy on theory, but in this chapter I'm going to show you how to apply that theory directly. I want you to understand how you can use what you've learned to create a system that makes it easier to save more WHILE you spend more guilt-free.

'But I hate budgets,' you say. I get that. Nobody wants to spend their precious spare time crunching numbers in budget planners and reconciling bank accounts. You'd rather hit your favourite brunch spot with your mates, sipping a turmeric latte with just a sprinkle of cinnamon, or eating your favourite Persian marinated fetta cheese on smashed avo toast with the special olive oil and a side of field mushrooms. You see budgeting as a process that will force you to count every dollar, make drastic lifestyle sacrifices, and generally become a more boring human.

But budgeting doesn't have to be that way. And simply burying your head in the sand and hoping for the best won't get you the results you want. Remember: the sooner you take action, the easier it is to get what you want. The longer you neglect your saving and spending, the harder you'll have to work and the more sacrifices you'll need to make.

Imagine that for the next 10 years, you don't worry about sorting your savings. No budgets. No savings plan. No conscious spending. You just live in the moment and enjoy what you've got. Then you finally get your act together and decide to save.

At that point, you do what I mentioned last chapter: you invest $10 each day into an account for 20 years, and it grows to around $175k. For only the cost of a couple of cups of coffee each day ($3650 over a year), that's a pretty good result, right?

The best time to take action was 10 years ago. The second best time is today.

But what about the alternative where you decide to take action and get started now? You invest your money for a total of 30 years, and (assuming the same returns and inputs) your investment is now worth over $460k. You end up with more than double the amount at the end.

Which outcome would you prefer?

And it gets better. Remember: if you started 20 years earlier (i.e. investing for a total of 40 years), your investment would be worth over $1.1m. The power of time makes a *huge* difference to the results you get.

This is why it's so important to get started. The best time to take action was 10 years ago. The second best time is today.

In this example, you're only saving $10 per day, which might be your limit. But there's a direct relationship between how much you save and the end results you get. So if you can manage to save double the amount, you can expect to have twice as much at the end. Saving $20 per day would mean you ended up with $350k, $920k, or $2.2m over 20, 30 and 40 years respectively. And pulling out all the stops to save $40 per day? This could result in final savings of $700k, $1.84m, or $4.4m over 20, 30 and 40 years respectively. Not bad right?

The problem is that most people can't find the extra money to save or invest. A good saving, spending and banking strategy can make this possible. When you get your saving strategy right, you can squeeze more money out of your current situation, 'creating' more money to save and/or invest.

Without a solid strategy and system, on the other hand, you'll be trapped in the constant 'juggle' of shuffling money from one place to another to cover your expenses, spending on credit and then cutting back to pay it down, and not growing your savings and investments at the rate you want.

So why is it so hard to get on top of your savings?

After helping hundreds of different people with their saving, spending and banking I've found there are a couple of myths that stop people from getting the results they want. I want to cover them here so you understand how to avoid falling into these traps.

Myth #1 'Figuring this out is easy'

The people I meet through my Financial Advice work have their finances in varying shapes. Some are in a complete mess with no structure at all, while others have a system they've been using to drive pretty good results. Some have done well by putting together tips and tactics from various sources. The most successful ones normally have a process where they review their progress and check what's worked and what hasn't. Then they adjust what they do to make success easier over time.

If you're like most young professionals, you probably think saving money should be easy, and that you should be able to do it yourself. You're an effective person who achieves and enjoys success. You're good at your job. You can manage people. You can balance your work, health and relationships. You're good at managing your time, and playing politics in the office. Maybe you can even cook …

In other words, you think you should be able to easily do anything you put your mind towards. So saving should be a cinch, right?

What most people don't realise is that true savings success takes years of time, effort and energy. People who achieve it spend a *lot* of time thinking about and managing their money. When we chat, they tell me they'd like to be able to get these results WITHOUT having to spend so much time thinking about money. And even the people who've been most successful doing this themselves still weren't spending and saving as effectively as they could have been.

Over the last six years or so, I've built the foundation for most of my work with clients around their savings strategy. And in the early stages of working with them, I now focus heavily on helping them with their saving and spending to make this foundation rock solid.

True savings takes years of time, effort and energy.

During this time, I've developed a system by testing what works and what doesn't, exploring any issues or roadblocks that come up, solving problems, and then refining and improving the system. After five years of working on this system day in, day out, it now works so well that it doesn't need to be refined any further.

I created the system because figuring this stuff out by yourself is hard. It will take up a lot of time and energy. It will be stressful. And unless you're a personal finance genius, or you want to spend five years figuring out your own system, you won't get the same results as you would from following mine. And let's face it, nobody wants to spend their nights and weekends crunching numbers in a spreadsheet, then analysing the results, tweaking payments and looking at the best apps and tools to manage their money.

Saving is *not* easy. You've already learnt how your psychology and decision-making processes have stacked the odds against you. Your personal finances are more complex today than they've ever been in the past. Don't fall into the trap of thinking you should figure this out yourself, or you'll end up frustrated, give up, and won't get the results you otherwise could.

Myth #2 'You have to count every dollar'

When I start talking to my clients about their saving and spending, they get a little nervous. Most people think that managing their money better means counting every dollar they spend and generally cutting back on their lifestyle.

But a good saving and spending plan doesn't need to mean drastic cuts to your lifestyle. It doesn't even have to mean cutting out a single thing that's important to you. You don't have to give up your turmeric latte, smashed avo, or cheat meals from Foodora on the couch. You definitely don't have to

> **A good saving and spending plan doesn't need to mean drastic cuts to your lifestyle.**

become 'that person' who analyses the dinner bill when they go out with mates and then splits everything down to the last cent.

Managing your spending and saving well simply means prioritising the things you most enjoy, and ruthlessly cutting out any spending that doesn't give you real value. It's so easy for low-value costs to creep into your spending, and they're often responsible for a lot of the 'leakage' that holds you back from getting the things you really want. Cutting out these low-value costs frees up cash to be directed to other areas.

Today it's easier than ever before to spend money without thinking. This is what I call 'unconscious spending', and it's responsible for a huge amount of leakage. The first step to avoid unconscious spending is to list out your ideal spending strategy. Think about what you'd ideally like to spend your money on. This also gets you thinking about where you've been spending your money in the past, which is often an eye-opening experience.

Every time I guide people through this process, they realise they've been mindlessly spending money on stuff that doesn't bring them real value. EVERY SINGLE TIME. This process of listing your spending forces you to understand where your money's going, and assess how much value you're getting out of each item.

Once you realise how much you're spending on different things, you can often identify expenses that you can painlessly eliminate without impacting your quality of life or general happiness levels. Your spending plan should be driven by what's important to you, and you don't need to cut anything that brings you value or happiness.

A good spending plan is all about prioritising the things you value most and reducing or eliminating everything else. But you're in control. You choose the priorities, and you control the outcomes. Once your priorities are set, you no longer need to count dollars. You just need to stick to your strategy.

And yes, I know this last point can seem impossible at times, but don't stress. I'm going to show you exactly how you can make it easy to stick to your strategy once it's set.

Unfortunately, the odds are against you

The way we manage money today is very different from the way we managed it in the past. It's getting easier and easier to spend money, and more and more complex to save and get ahead. Cash withdrawals from ATMs today are at an all-time low because more people are choosing to transact electronically with credit and debit cards, and mobile and 'tap and go' payments.

It's getting easier and easier to spend money, and more and more complex to save and get ahead.

I've said before that there's a surprisingly high amount of psychology in the decision-making processes that drive how we manage our money. The more I learn about these processes, the more I realise that the way most people manage their day-to-day saving and spending dooms them to financial mediocrity at best. It leads to years of slow progress, frustration, and eventually having to settle for money and lifestyle outcomes of a much lower standard than they want (and deserve).

I've also mentioned earlier that several high-profile economists, behavioural psychologists, researchers and Nobel prize winners have studied money psychology and decision-making processes. It's no surprise you're not told about their findings on your new credit card application form.

I must admit: before I started researching this book, I wasn't aware of just how many studies there *were* on the psychology of modern money management. But I've seen the results in practice. Over years of helping people with their money, I've seen what works and what doesn't. When I stumbled onto these studies as part of researching this book, everything started to make sense.

I never knew why the banking system we followed with our clients worked—and frankly, I didn't really care. All that mattered to me was that it *did* work. But if only I'd known about this sooner, I probably could have saved myself a bunch of time by applying these principles to the work we were doing. Live and learn…

We've already covered your psychological biases and decision-making flaws in previous chapters. Now I want to show you how you can use these factors to your advantage. Below I've put together some hacks you can apply directly to your banking to make it easier to save. Then I'm going to show you a system you can use to incorporate the hacks into your everyday money management.

Brain Hack #1—Create small barriers

We've already discussed how the smallest of barriers can have a big impact on your decision-making processes. In Chapter 1, we covered the study that showed how placing chocolates a few steps away from office workers in a cupboard vs on their desks in plain sight resulted in drastically reduced consumption. The same principle can apply to your spending.

Most people have all their money in one account, or—even more commonly—do most of their spending on a credit card. If you do this, you don't have to think about how much you're spending or whether that spending fits with what you ideally want to happen. In other words, there's no barrier between you and breaking your budget—so you spend more.

Placing small barriers between you and what you don't want to happen makes it surprisingly easier to get the things you do want. You can achieve this by separating the money you plan to spend from the money you want to save; and then separating out the money you want to spend on different types of costs, e.g. your bills and your holiday fund. I've found this is even *more* powerful if you use a different bank for your everyday spending money. It won't stop you from spending, because you still have access to all of your cash, but it will force you to think.

You'll have to actively choose to work outside of the plan you've set, and make a conscious choice to break your budget. This will force you to think twice; and when you do, you'll more often than not choose the right thing.

This is something that's helped me personally, and helped many of the people I've worked with to stay on track more easily. It will significantly increase your chances of getting the results you want.

Harness the power of barriers to drive better saving results.

Harness the power of barriers to drive better saving results.

Brain Hack #2 — Your willpower is a limited resource

In Chapter 1, we spoke about the concept of willpower depletion and decision fatigue. To recap: the research proves that when you have to 'spend' your willpower on trying hard to avoid doing something (e.g. resisting the temptation of food), you'll give up much more easily on another task requiring willpower. This means that when your limited 'willpower credits' are spent, you're less able to use willpower in other areas and more likely to give up.

This also applies to your spending. You'll inevitably come across times where you have to resist the temptation to spend money. Everybody has wants. We've all been in the situation where we're doing something online, e.g. watching cat videos on YouTube or researching a work project. Then, suddenly it's like Google reads our minds and blasts us with advertisements for something we want.

The ads you see might be for an inflatable banana lounge for your next beach day, the new clothes you were just checking out from your favourite website, or that 83-pocket cable organiser with the compact compartment and security zip that comes in three awesome colours. Regardless, you really want this stuff, but you know you can't afford it if you want to hit your savings targets.

It takes *willpower* to resist this temptation.

To avoid suffering the consequences of 'willpower depletion', set up your banking in a way that doesn't require your willpower to work. Harnessing the power of barriers WILL stop you from splurging when you know you shouldn't. If your spending money is separated and just that one additional step away in a different bank, you reduce temptation because spending isn't actually possible at that moment.

You get to move on, and afterwards realise that your cupboard is already full of clothes, your tech cables are already organised, and you have that holiday coming up—and, oh yeah, you DON'T REALLY NEED ANY OF THAT ANYWAY.

Brain Hack #3—Stick to 'Defaults'

We've already discussed how we humans have this in-built tendency to stick to our default settings and resist change. We get busy, distracted and sometimes even lazy, and end up going back to whatever our baseline setting is. To harness this with your saving and spending, set your default to get you the outcomes you want.

You shouldn't have to decide how much to save, where to save it, or manually move your money. If you set up your banking to automatically transfer the money you want into the right places at the right times to save the amount you want, you'll get your tendency to stick to your defaults working for you instead of against you.

Make success your default and you can happily give in to your human tendencies, knowing everything's on track.

Long story short—you need a system

I'm a systems guy. As I've said before: I feel that most things in life can be broken down into a process. Your saving and spending is no different, but this sort of thinking doesn't come naturally.

An effective saving and spending strategy is important. But an awesome plan by itself won't get you great results. You also need a system that supports the strategy and makes it easy. Most importantly, you need one that'll make your saving and spending wants happen.

Having to make too many extra decisions about how you manage your money can get overwhelming. Like Lola in Chapter 1, you get paid into one account and have to shuffle your money from that account to another one. You pay this bill. Then you make sure there's money for your rent. You pay off your credit card. Then you pay some money onto your personal loan. You ask yourself how much you're supposed to be saving. And where should it be going again ...?

No wonder you throw your hands in the air, put this huge juggle into the too-hard basket, and go back to the cat videos while hoping for the best. The more choices you need to make, the more likely you are to get off track.

The diagram below shows the system I use to help clients automate and manage their saving and spending.

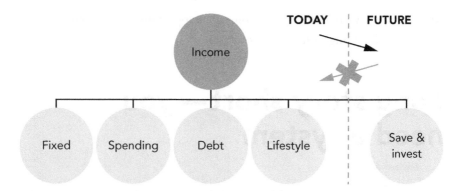

I've found this system can help anyone to save more while spending guilt-free on the things that are important to them. With this structure, you know exactly where your money should be at any time; and by following it, you can automate payments so they flow without any input of time or energy (or stress).

The average adult makes over 30000 decisions every single day, so you don't need another choice to make.

Whether it's a banking strategy like the one above, an investment plan, or a debt repayment strategy, automate wherever possible to reduce your time input and free up your mental energy to focus on other things. The average adult makes over 30000 decisions every single day, so you don't need another choice to make.

How to save MORE and spend BETTER

Next, I want to take you through how you can harness the power of this system. In this section, we're going to cover how to set up an automated banking strategy that will help you to save MORE and spend BETTER. This process follows four steps:

1. Sort your day-to-day spending.

2. Choose year-on-year results.

3. Automate your banking.

4. Make your savings work.

Go to [bit.ly/GUStools] to download the spreadsheet I use with clients to get started on sorting out your own process today.

Step 1. Sort your day-to-day spending

Knowing what money you have coming in and going out is the first step toward setting up a rock-solid saving and spending strategy. I know budgets often seem confusing, boring and a waste of time. But this is because they're usually done in isolation, and not as part of a process. If you get this process right, you'll be able to ditch the budget—you'll only ever need to adjust things when your situation changes.

For this to work well the first time you do it, you need to think through everything you currently spend your money on. You also need to think about all the things you WANT to spend your money on. This means listing out all your day-to-day costs, as well as any infrequent expenses like travel and holidays, car insurance and maintenance, Christmas gifts, and your yearly subscription to the Newtown Taco Appreciation Society (or other random social collective).

Ignoring these expenses will mean the money is missing when you need it. This is one of the most common budgeting mistakes.

Pro Tip

Include an extra amount in your budget for unexpected expenses, as these always come up. The right number here depends on your income and spending, but I typically recommend between $1k-$5k per annum.

Pro Tip

The only costs you should include in your budget are your ongoing annual costs, not any one-off expenses. For example, if you have a one-off expense of $5k for a big holiday or a new tech upgrade that will happen in the next 12 months but then not in each following year, it shouldn't go into your everyday budget. Instead, include this as a one-off cost (more on this below).

This process will help you to see where your money is going. Once it's all down on paper (or—my preference—in a spreadsheet) look at what's left over. This is your savings 'surplus'. Note that this number should be positive. If it's not, don't give up now—this is completely normal, and most people I've done this with (including myself) start with a negative number. It just means a little more work is needed.

Looking at all your costs is an eye-opening exercise that will get you thinking about how much value you're getting from your spending. Remember that 'value' means something that brings you real enjoyment and contributes to your overall happiness. These are typically things that make your life easier, provide you with amazing experiences, or make you feel good about yourself. They might be donating to your favourite charity or shouting yourself a manipedi (or, in my case, a beard trim at my favourite barber shop).

Things that fulfil a momentary desire or add to your clutter, on the other hand, are usually NOT expenses that bring real value.

Prioritising is critical to being happy with your spending as well as your saving. So review where you're spending, and prioritise the things that bring you value. It's common for expenses that bring you little real value to creep into your budget. Ruthlessly cut these costs to free up money to spend in other areas or save and invest. Prioritising is critical to being happy with your spending as well as your saving. There's no one approach that's right for everyone, because the right spending plan for you includes the things that are most important to YOU.

You should also be happy with the amount of surplus you create each week/fortnight/month, and what this means for your other money and lifestyle goals. Your goal for your saving and spending strategy should be to find the perfect balance between spending enough to give you the 'today lifestyle' you want, while saving enough for the 'future lifestyle' you want. This is a circular process; and to get the best outcome possible, you'll have to return to this step once you've completed the steps below.

Note: people often ask me what sort of percentages they should be spending in each of these areas, i.e. saving 20 per cent, spending 30 per cent, lifestyle 15 per cent, etc.

I'm against applying one percentage 'rule' that's right for everyone. I think the right split between your different spending areas depends on the point you're at now and the results, targets or outcomes you're trying to get from your money. This will often change over time. Don't fall into the trap of thinking you should be following some expert's or blogger's fool-proof, dummy-proof, life-proof strategy.

Choose the setup that's right to get YOU the things YOU want.

Step 2. Choose year-on-year results

The next step is to lay out any upcoming one-off expenses and/or changes in your income. I call this your 'lifestyle spending'. The name is a little confusing, because lifestyle spending isn't granola at your favourite cafe or an afternoon at the day spa. It's your bigger ticket spending that happens irregularly on top of your day-to-day spending.

This sort of spending might be $10k you want for a big trip next year, buying a new car, or doing some renovations. Changes in your income might be due to taking time out of the workforce for children, changing jobs or career paths, or launching a business.

If you just sort your day-to-day spending without also providing for this lifestyle spending, you won't have enough money to pay for the latter when it crops up. This will force you to cut the expenses or dip into your savings or money allocated to other areas (e.g. investing or debt reduction). That will then throw your strategy off track and cause unnecessary stress and frustration.

The process of choosing your lifestyle spending should be fun. Think through your bucket list. Dream big. Lay out all the things you'd love to spend your money on and how much they cost.

When you've got your list, compare:

- Your current savings.
- How much surplus you'll have each year from your new budget (i.e. extra savings).
- How your savings balance will change with your big ticket expenses or other changes to your income.

At this point, you'll likely need to do some prioritising around your timeline and the spending that's most important to you. Sometimes this will mean reviewing your budget and changing how much you spend on each priority. At other times, it may mean tweaking the timing of certain expenses.

Sadly, this is a little less fun than mapping out your bucket list. But once you've got it right, the result is a spending and saving strategy that not only provides for the spending you want most today, but that also covers the bigger spending you want to do in the future (and any changes to your situation over time).

This is essential for making smart decisions with your savings, and helps you confidently invest.

> ## Pro Tip
>
> If you want to spend money on any big ticket items or on lifestyle choices like time out of the workforce, you need to plan for them. This is the step where all these things should be included, so you can move forward with full confidence knowing all the spending you want to do is taken care of.

Step 3. Automate your banking

There are only so many 'types' of expenses out there, and they're all important. If you can classify your expenses and group them together, it allows you to provide for them at the right time. Grouping these expenses will also allow you to automate your banking, which is critical for a good saving strategy.

The expense categories I use are:

- Fixed costs—rent, bills and all regular direct debit type expenses.
- Spending—everyday pocket money, food, entertainment and general expenses.
- Debt—any personal debt, investment loan or mortgage costs.
- Lifestyle—travel and big ticket expenses.
- Future—all savings or investments.

Classify your costs from the budgeting exercise above into similar (or identical) categories, and you're ready to automate. Once this is complete, I typically suggest running multiple bank accounts to keep your money in these various categories in line with the banking system below.

This will mean your bills and any debt will all be paid automatically, and you'll receive spending money into your everyday account each week for day-to-day costs. Meanwhile, your travel fund will be building up for your next holiday, and your savings (or investments) will automatically happen.

It also becomes simple to track your money, and eliminates your need for number crunching in spreadsheets or using spending tracking apps or tools. You can then get on with what's important to you, knowing your money is taken care of and that you're getting the results you want.

Once you've completed this, the only account you should need to think about is your everyday spending account and—occasionally—your lifestyle/travel fund balance. The rest of your accounts will take care of themselves.

When this happens, any money that hits your everyday spending account becomes 'guilt-free' spending. Because you know everything else has already been taken care of, you can spend this money on anything you want. If you want to spend it all on new clothes, a shopping spree on eBay, or a massive booze-up with your mates, no problem. You can spend like money's going out of fashion, knowing your account will be refilled next week.

Pro Tip

Think about using one bank for your income, fixed costs, travel/lifestyle and savings, and a different bank for your everyday spending. This harnesses the power of barriers to drive better results.

Step 4. Make your savings work

Once you've nailed your saving and spending system to a point you're happy with, automated your banking, and know what you've got to work with, the next step is to do something smart with the money you're saving.

Once again, the right thing is different for everyone because it depends on where you're at now, how your situation will change over time, and what's important to you.

Regardless, though, you need to get your money working hard for you.

Pro Tip

The most common—and most effective—options are keeping your money in cash savings (good if you're going to need to spend the money soon), or investing in either share type investments, property or your superannuation/retirement account. Explore these options and figure out which is right for you: they're all covered in detail in the third section of this book.

The benefits of this savings system

Your saving and spending strategies will drive your money results. They'll dictate how fast your savings grow, when your lifestyle goals are achievable, what you should invest in and how much, and how quickly you can set up the future you want.

If you want to be successful with money, you *have* to get this right. If you invest time now into setting a clear strategy, backed up by a solid system, your money foundations will be in place. You can then get on with the important things, knowing you're making the progress you want. And the best part? It will all just happen, ticking away in the background without you having to think about it.

Following this process and setting up your banking system this way will set you up for savings success. That's because it harnesses the power of your money decision-making and psychology to work FOR you instead of AGAINST you. It will take a little time and effort to set up, but once it's up and running, it'll be clear, simple and easy to manage. It will save you a bunch of time, which is important because if something requires too much effort from you to make it work, you're much more likely to give up.

This system is also easy to track. There's no need for complex, time-consuming apps or spending trackers. The system will just work. Because you've set your default strategy for saving success, you'll simply know that if nothing happens, then everything's working. You'll know that you're saving the amount you want, and have the money you want to spend on the things that are important to you when they come up.

Following this process and setting up your banking system this way will set you up for savings success.

And because your system is automated, you won't have to spend any willpower to save money. Instead, you can simply get on with your spending, knowing everything is provided for. This will help you to reserve your valuable willpower for use in other areas where it will bring you even more benefits.

PUTTING IT ALL TOGETHER

Saving money sounds so simple, but it really isn't. It is important, though. And it's the first big step towards getting smart with money. Get this right and everything else will flow and become so much easier.

How much you can save is the factor that has the biggest impact on your money results over time. You can't do a budget and hope for the best—it just won't work. Time and time again, I've seen the power of having a good process and system around saving, spending and banking as I've helped people to build the system I've outlined in this chapter.

I know I'm repeating myself here, but the results are so powerful that it's worth it. My clients use this system, and on average they save over 35 per cent of their income, which is more than seven times the Australian national average of 4.7 per cent. This system works. But it won't just happen. You need to give this your attention and focus, and then put in the work.

And, like Big Kev would say on a dodgy 90s infomercial, 'But wait, there's more.' On top of saving you more so you end up with more money, a good structure around your saving and spending allows you to plan with your money. It's almost impossible to get money-smart if you don't have a good handle on how much you're spending and saving.

If you try to invest without this structure, you won't know how much money to invest. If you need money you've invested, you can also be forced to sell investments at the wrong time, losing money as a result. And if you want to buy property, you won't know how much you can comfortably afford without being forced to make lifestyle sacrifices. If you're clear on your spending, saving and banking, on the other hand, planning in other areas becomes much easier and more effective.

So if you want to save, invest, buy property or just spend guilt-free, you need to know how much you have to work with, and how much you need for your spending and lifestyle wants.

The good news is that you can get smart around the choices you make. When you do, you'll be able to take action with confidence, knowing your plan is solid. We'll jump into planning in the next section of this book, but for now you need to nail down your saving and spending before you can implement any of the learnings we'll cover in that section.

Like anything money-related, the key is to get on top of your spending and saving sooner rather than later, but I know it's not always that easy. Learn from the mistakes that I and many others before you have made, and hack your thinking to force yourself to spend on the right things and squeeze more money out of your income.

The psychological biases that affect your savings are subtle, but their impacts are huge; so use these insights to your advantage. Take control of your spending and saving today and you'll save faster, spend guilt-free, and simplify your money management.

SECTION 2
STRATEGY

In the first section, I covered your money 'structure', which is the foundation of your finances. A good structure will make it easy to save more money as well as manage your money on a day-to-day basis. Then, once your structure is in place, you'll know what money you have to work with. The next step after that is to get smart about what you do with your money to make it grow.

In other words, it's time to get smart with your strategy.

A good strategy will allow you to get the best results for YOU with your money. To create a smart strategy, you want to understand the options available to you, their impact, and the benefits and any risks or downsides of each. This will help you choose the combination of options and strategies that will get the best results for you.

A solid planning framework will also give you clear goals to work toward, which is important to keep you motivated and on track. Taking the easy option with money normally means getting off track and spending everything you earn (or more). But having clear targets and a timeline for when you'll get there will remind you why you're doing what you're doing. As we talked about in Chapter 4, saving a bunch of money is hard—but saving the same amount of money for something you really want and can see yourself achieving over a timeline you're happy with is much easier.

Another advantage of getting smart with your strategy is that it allows you to manage risk. Understanding the risks you face means you can choose whether to accept, eliminate or avoid those risks. Mapping out your strategy also allows you to avoid one of the biggest and most commonly ignored risks, which is lifestyle risk.

So in this section, we'll cover how to plan with your money and set up that smart strategy. We'll talk about how to prioritise the things that are most important to you, and how to create a plan to make them happen. We'll go through how to manage risk in your strategy, how to set good targets and goals around your money, and a process to set up a smart strategy.

Note: In this section, I use the words 'strategy', 'plan', and 'path' interchangeably. They're all the same, and just mean an overall strategy for your money.

By the end of this section, you'll be across all the key elements needed to create a rock-solid strategy that will take you from where you are today to the results you want into the future. Then you'll be all set to jump into investments.

But first ... the strategy.

CHAPTER 5

You can't have it all

'If you fail to plan, you plan to fail.' We've all heard that famous Benjamin Franklin saying. Everyone knows it. The most successful companies, organisations and individuals plan. We see the results and hear about the benefits. Some of us do it as part of our job.

Benjamin Franklin's quote is one of the most cited of all time. But so few people plan around their money. So what's stopping *you*?

Before you answer this, it may help to realise that there are two key stages you'll go through with your money.

- **The 'building' stage** of your money life cycle involves growing your assets, savings and investments. It's where you don't yet have enough to turn off the income tap. While you might enjoy your job, at this point in your money journey you're effectively a slave to your income because if it stopped, you wouldn't be able to live the way you want.
- **The 'spending' stage** comes once you've built your assets and investment income to the point you don't rely on your employment income to support your living expenses any more. When you're starting to get

smart with your money, you'll likely need to spend a bit of time in the building phase before you get to the spending phase. But unless you want to live a life you don't enjoy now just to make your future self rich, you should enjoy the journey as well as the destination.

Of course, you could get to the spending phase much faster if you were happy to spend your 20s, 30s and 40s eating nothing but baked beans, sitting in a dark room with no TV, and never leaving your house except to work in a soulless job you hate and that pays well. But to me (and most of the people I've helped), this would equate to a waste of life, and is too expensive a price to pay for an early retirement.

Instead, you need to find balance. A good plan shows you how you can get from where you are today to where you want to be in the future, while enjoying your lifestyle along the way. Yes, that's right, **while enjoying your lifestyle along the way**. Remember that a money plan doesn't need to mean cutting back your spending, sacrificing down your holiday and entertainment budgets, and basically taking out all the fun stuff.

The goal of a smart money strategy is to get more money. You'll need to prioritise to get there, as we discussed in the previous section. But the most important thing you can do when you set up your strategy — and the thing that will give you the best chance of success — is to find a balance you're happy with between your personal and financial objectives. Then you can live well now WHILE you set up the future you want.

It's so important to enjoy the path as well as the destination. And solid planning will help you to choose the money AND lifestyle outcomes you want, and work them into a strategy where you can have both.

I'm not saying you can have *every* possible financial and lifestyle outcome you want. For most people (myself included), that would be close to impossible. But the process of setting up a clear plan will allow you to prioritise what's most important. It will help you to choose which money outcomes are most important to you, which lifestyle outcomes you want to focus on first, and how to set a timeline to achieve everything else.

This is powerful stuff, and shouldn't be taken lightly.

Not surprisingly, when you make lifestyle a key focus of your money strategy, it becomes easier to stick to your plan. Because you get to enjoy yourself as you plan out your enjoyable lifestyle targets as well as your money goals, you'll be much more likely to stick to your strategy. If, on the other hand, you just focus on money outcomes, you'll find it tough to stick to your plan because you probably won't enjoy yourself enough.

When you make lifestyle a key focus of your money strategy, it becomes easier to stick to your plan.

I was working with a client recently (I'll call him Hudson) who had two big goals. He wanted to go on a three-month trip to South America, and he also really wanted to get into the property market. He had some savings, but when we looked at where he was heading on his current path, he wouldn't have enough money to hit both targets in a timeframe he was happy with.

Hudson was keen to buy property. He'd been living in a five-bedroom shared house in Sydney for the last six years; and while he'd enjoyed it, he was a little over communal living. He'd moved into this place with some mates from university, and it had started out well. Over time, though, his original housemates had been replaced with others further outside his circle of friends. The shine of shared living had dimmed over time: he now wanted his own space, and was ready for a change.

But he was also set on South America. A good mate of his had gone there about a year ago and brought back some *amazing* stories. He'd told Hudson about trekking through Patagonia in a snowstorm, sunrise over Ipanema Beach in Rio de Janeiro, scuba diving in Colombia, and trekking Machu Picchu.

Hudson had started doing some research, and now had a few ideas of his own. He was a bit of an adrenaline junkie, so he wanted to kitesurf through the Salar de Uyuni in Bolivia, go white water rafting through the rapids of Ecuador, and go skydiving over the Nazca Lines in Peru.

When it comes to plotting out your money and lifestyle goals, anything is possible. You can use certain levers to get anything you want (within reason). For example, you can:

- make more money
- spend less on your everyday costs
- save more
- cut your travel budget
- invest more
- invest with more risk
- sell the cat
- sell a kidney.

Okay, so the last two options are clearly not serious (please don't rush out and start selling your organs *or* your fur babies). But the other options there are really the only things you can do to jostle your ability to get the things you want. And they're the same for everyone.

Pro Tip

When you're setting up any money strategy, think through which of the items on the list above you're comfortable with, which you'd consider, and which are completely off the table. The answers are different for everyone, and there's no one choice that works best.

Some involve more pain, some more stress, and some will be totally off the table for you. Only when you understand your levers, how to use them, and how you feel about their impact can you really start to consider your options.

Hudson's two goals were big ones. We knew they'd both involve a bunch of costs, but I also knew they were possible. I know that what *you* want is possible too, even without knowing where you are now with your money.

As Hudson set up his plan, we talked through each of the available levers to explore what might be possible. And we found he had a few good options, plus a couple that were absolutely non-negotiable.

Hudson wanted to achieve these two goals without taking a bunch of crazy risks or making too many lifestyle sacrifices. He also didn't want to drastically reduce his day-to-day spending. We were running out of levers, and both he and I were wondering how this was going to work.

But after some further discussion, Hudson discovered it was possible to take a secondment through his employer, which would involve a bit of a pay bump. While he didn't find this ideal, it was still one of the more appealing options. So he agreed to explore further.

As you can guess from his goal, Hudson was a mad traveller. He'd travelled around most of the world (except for South America), and a big line item in his spending plan was his annual holiday. After talking it through further, he decided if he could have this big dream trip to South America relatively soon, he'd be happy to carve some funds out of his shorter-term holiday budget. He wasn't super-excited about this at first, but agreed it was worth exploring.

So we went through the process of plotting out his options. And we found that making these two changes meant his bigger targets became realistically achievable within the timeframe he wanted.

Hudson was stoked; and once he saw that his important goals were achievable, he was more prepared to accept some short-term 'pain' to get to them. So he went to see his boss to discuss taking the secondment and got it.

The plan was in motion.

The photos Hudson took on his South America trip renewed my own passion for América del Sur. He managed to tick all the adrenaline activities off his list, plus a couple of extra ones for good measure. He also said the experience opened his eyes, and even gave him an idea for starting a future business.

Then when he returned, he focused in on his work and received a promotion (with a healthy pay bump) shortly afterwards. So he's now shopping for properties and set on this goal with laser focus.

This combination of changes wouldn't be right for everyone. Not everyone is prepared to take a secondment and move away from where they live, or cut their short-term travel budget. But for Hudson, this was the right way to get what he wanted.

To get the most out of planning, the first step is to understand what's possible, and the levers you can use to get what you want. The next step is to think about the impact of pulling each of those levers on your money and lifestyle goals, and whether you're happy with that impact.

Pro Tip

Sometimes when you're planning, you have to loop back around, revisit and re-prioritise what's important to you. That's okay. In fact, it's completely normal. It will help you find balance between your money and lifestyle wants, and then build an action plan to make them both happen.

Remember: there are no 'right' decisions. There's only what's right for you.

There are no 'right' decisions. There's only what's right for you.

Don't be fooled into thinking there's one path you need to follow that sets up your money to give you the lifestyle you want. You need to prioritise the things that are most important to you. The result is a path that's right for YOU and one YOU will be happy to follow.

No such thing as a 'good' choice

When you're trying to set up your money strategy, you'll probably hear stories or advice from other people about what you should do to get the best results. Just like we talked about in Chapter 1, your colleague will tell you how they're making big money investing in property. The barista at your favourite cafe will tell you how they're crushing it buying bitcoin. Your uncle will insist you should save your money in cold, hard cash and sew it into your mattress because it just makes sense cash is getting harder to come by and the nuclear winter is coming…

And again, chances are that each person will swear by their suggested strategy, telling you how it worked for them and how it would work for you. They'll probably also tell you how someone else made a bunch of money going down this path, and why it's a 'no brainer'.

But could it be this easy?

It's true that you need to do *something* smart with your money if your ideal lifestyle doesn't involve working forever. Investments are a tool that can provide you with income, and so reduce your dependence on employment income. But great investments WILL NOT make you rich. Nor will they mean you can retire early. In fact, having great investments won't even guarantee you don't make mistakes.

I had a client—let's call him Dylan—with some mates who were professional investors. Those mates had been working in investments for more than 10 years, and were into some pretty complicated investment strategies involving complex products.

Meanwhile, Dylan was earning a good income, and was managing to save a solid amount with each pay cheque. He knew he should be doing something smarter with his savings, and he was getting hammered with tax.

The problem was that he didn't know *what* to do, and was worried about making the wrong decision.

After talking with his mates just before we met, Dylan decided to put most of his savings into a fairly complex, long-duration (three-year) investment. The prospects for the investment looked good, and he was eagerly awaiting his pay day. He watched its progress, and everything seemed to be going well, so both he and his mates were very happy.

This all sounds great, right? Well sort of.

The long and short of it was that Dylan ended up smashing it at his job and getting a good pay bump. He'd known this was on the cards, and had been working towards it for a while. That higher income, coupled with a few other strategies we'd set up for him, meant he ended up in a position to buy his first investment property much sooner than he thought possible. But here's the thing…

All these results on their own are great things. Investments doing well. More savings. Less tax. More income. Ability to buy property. BUT because Dylan was effectively locked into his original long-term investment, he couldn't exit it and get back the money he'd needed for a deposit on the property he wanted to buy.

This put him in a difficult situation with only two options forward. First, he could exit his long-term investment, lose the money he'd made AND pay a hefty penalty fee, which would allow him to buy the property. Or, he could ride out the investment and delay buying property. Neither option was ideal.

Dylan chose the second option and held off on buying the property. Unfortunately, with increases in Sydney property values over this time, this option ended up costing him a packet in terms of lost earnings. His longer-term investments have since matured and made him money, but he's now looking at higher house prices and has had to settle for getting much less property for his money.

People get caught up thinking a particular investment is objectively 'good'. But if you don't think about how it fits in with all the other aspects of your money strategy, you can run into the same issue Dylan experienced. In reality, any investment can be 'good' or 'bad'. Whether it's **good for you** depends on your situation, lifestyle and financial wants, and how your situation is likely to change over time.

Dylan caused problems for himself because he didn't think about how his wants or situation could change over time. In this case, a fairly high-returning, tax-effective investment ended up being a 'bad' investment. If he'd built more flexibility into his strategy, he could have made more money.

If flexibility could provide a significant benefit to you, then an investment that's less tax-effective or one with a lower return might be 'good' for you at a certain point in time. If you're in a different situation though, it could easily be a 'bad' investment.

Pro Tip

To avoid trouble when you're making money choices, think about how your decision fits with not only your situation today, but also with your current plans for the future and how your situation might change over time.

Plot out how your situation might change, and consider setting up an overall plan for your money which includes the lifestyle or personal goals and targets that are important to you. This will help you avoid choices that will slow down your progress or hold you back.

Getting your strategy right from the start will hugely boost your outcomes now and in the future. You'll feel more confident and motivated. It will also have a massive impact on the money progress you make. It's your strategy, your plan, that drives the right decisions for you.

It's your strategy, your plan, that drives the right decisions for you.

Dylan's story shows that different options have different risks and benefits. The same option can be better for some people, but be a disaster for others. What's right for you will be different to what's right for your old mate down the street.

If you plan your money strategy effectively, you can ensure you only include options that will fit with both your situation now and any changes to that situation over time. This will reduce your chances of making mistakes or running into roadblocks that will slow you down or set you back. You'll also be less stressed about your strategy, because you'll know you've managed your risk, and you'll be much more likely to get better results and outcomes over time.

Again, there are no 'good' choices. There are only choices that are good *for you*. Plan well, and the right choices for you will become clear.

PUTTING IT ALL TOGETHER

You should never have to settle. But if you're like most people, you probably want to do more things than your money will allow in the timeframe you'd ideally like. This means you need to prioritise. Making sacrifices is never ideal, but you can't opt out.

If you don't actively make a choice, the choice will be made for you. If you choose to bury your head in the sand and continue enjoying everything you want today with no consideration of the future, you're choosing to prioritise your today spending and lifestyle; and as a result, your future self will suffer.

The 'building' phase of your strategy is key to making sure that you have enough money to do all the things you want when the 'spending' phase kicks in. If you don't, you'll be forced to make sacrifices.

It's only by thinking ahead and planning that you can understand whether you're happy with where you'll end up. The planning process will also help you to choose better paths to get where you want to be. Seeing everything laid out will help you to prioritise.

You *can* have it all. But you can't have it all right now. If you have to make any sacrifices, make sure they're the things you value least.

CHAPTER 6

Know your knowns and unknowns

No-one wants to be seen as stupid, and change is scary by its nature. So you put pressure on yourself to make good choices.

You want to do the right thing. You don't want to be 'that person'—the one everyone looks down on as though you should have known better. You don't want to feel that if only you'd taken the time to do this or that (or this and that), you could have avoided all this trouble. You don't want to be the one stressing that if you'd just chosen better, by now you'd be an epically Instafamous superstar doing paid product placements for your favourite health shakes and skincare products.

In other words, you want to be smart. And when you're making money choices, you don't want to do anything that will cause you problems or end up meaning you get left behind your peers, mates or family.

This fear is natural. But sometimes it can be responsible for the very things you're worried about.

For example, I've been working with a client, that I'll call Charlie, for a couple of years now. She was a young executive who was good at saving and had a solid savings account. She was paying a stack of tax on her income, and because all her savings went into a high-interest savings account, she paid extra tax on that too. Now she wanted to buy property; and although she already had enough savings to make it happen, she hadn't taken the leap.

I worked with Charlie to plan out her property purchase to fit with both her situation now and how that situation might change over time (see Chapter 5 for more about this). When we got into the numbers, we found that property fit her very comfortably without putting any pressure on her.

We also found that purchasing property was possible at a higher price point than Charlie had been thinking of—even allowing for risk, the unexpected and a likely temporary income reduction as she changed career direction. She ended up buying a great property, but when I investigated further, we realised she could have purchased the same property much sooner. She'd actually missed out on over $200k in lost growth by delaying her purchase.

If Charlie had taken action back when it was first possible, she'd be much further down the path to Instafamousness. Well maybe not quite, but she would have made a bunch of extra money that she could then have put to work to make her *more* money over time. So perhaps Instafamousness might have been on the cards after all...

I'm always curious about what drives the money choices people make, so I asked Charlie why it had taken her so long to get started. The reason was the very same I've heard from many others in the past: information overload.

As we covered in Chapter 3, information overload and analysis paralysis are very real factors that cause people to get stuck in the inaction trap, often for years. When you're caught by them, you hear too many different viewpoints, mixed messages and advice, so you get overwhelmed and do nothing.

But underneath the overload and paralysis lies fear—in particular, the fear of making the wrong choice or doing something that will cause you trouble. This fear is healthy because it stops you from making bad decisions. But it's important to not let fear stop you from making good decisions too.

Don't let fear stop you from making good decisions.

It's also important to get clear on the things you currently know about your situation and how that situation could change over time. AND you need to take the time to understand your unknowns, too, so they don't cause you trouble in the future.

This is where a smart strategy comes in.

When you're making a choice, setting your financial course, or changing the direction you're taking with your money, a solid plan helps you see how everything fits together. It forces you to build your knowledge and financial education around *all* the variables that impact the choice you're considering. It allows you to get comfortable with the direction you're taking because you know you've considered everything. This is most of the battle to reduce the fear that stops you from taking action.

Charlie told me later that fear had been holding her back, but that the planning process had eliminated that fear for her. It let her see how everything fit together. Then, once she had a plan in place and could see how buying property would work, she immediately felt empowered to take action.

Without a solid plan, you'll lack the confidence you need to take action.

You'll lack the confidence to make decisions when you should.

You'll also lack the confidence to make changes when you should.

And you'll lack the confidence to stick with your strategy when it's most important.

This is the power of planning. Get this right, and you'll eliminate your fear—just like Charlie did. You'll empower yourself to get started on building the momentum that's so important with money.

The biggest hidden risk most people overlook

Charlie was very sensible and risk-averse, with high fear levels. And because she didn't take the time to 'know her unknowns', she ended up sitting on the sidelines for longer than she should have. About half of the people I meet take this approach and wait longer than they should, trying to find the perfect time to act. But some people have the opposite problem. Their fear levels aren't high enough, so these people rush in before they understand all the risks they should be aware of.

When you're making money choices, you want to get the best result with the lowest level of risk. To do this, you need to understand that risk comes in many forms. There's investment risk, risk of the unexpected, and lifestyle risk.

To create your perfect money strategy, you need to understand which risks you face so you can manage them. You can't eliminate risk entirely—there are simply no risk-free money strategies. But you can choose which risks you're prepared to face, which you want to avoid, and which you can manage.

Another young professional couple, who I'll call Riley and Eve, were a couple who wanted to get ahead with their money while enjoying their lifestyle. Both in their early 30s, they worked hard and had built a solid savings balance. They were thinking about starting a family soon, and were sick of renting—so they also wanted to buy a place of their own.

They started looking at properties, and found a lovely two-bedroom place in Five Dock, just a few kilometres from the Sydney CBD. They were in a solid position with strong income, and plenty of savings capacity. They did some rough numbers around what they could afford, decided to take the leap, and managed to get the property they wanted for a price they loved. They were stoked and thought they were doing everything right.

Around a year later, they decided to have their first child; and Eve fell pregnant shortly afterwards. They were both super-excited about their future plans: Eve would have a year off work after their baby was born, and then she'd go back to work part-time for the next couple of years.

When they started running the numbers, though, they realised there was a problem. With their mortgage payments, living expenses and Eve's reduction in income, they were about to start going backwards quickly. It wouldn't be long until they'd spent all their savings.

That put them in a bind. They enjoyed their lifestyle: travelling, eating out and going to gigs. Eve in particular had a weakness for hipster cafes, and was guilty of filling her Insta account with shameless food photos. Her Instafollowers were growing…but their joint bank balance was going in the opposite direction.

After looking into their financials, Riley and Eve both realised some sacrifices were required. They simply couldn't afford to live the lifestyle they wanted without spending all their savings and then racking up additional debt. They didn't want to cut back on expenses or reduce their holiday budget, but they were running out of options.

So they did it. They carved money out of their holiday budget and cut down on gigs, and their restaurant budget also copped a blow. Their budget situation improved, and things started looking more positive.

But I've seen this situation a bunch of times before. When someone's forced to make drastic sacrifices and can no longer live the lifestyle they want, they start getting frustrated. It just isn't sustainable.

Riley and Eve kept cutting back for the next six months. Because they weren't happy with the money they now had for their entertainment allowance though, some of the costs they'd previously cut started creeping back into their spending.

And because their income was now limited, the extra spending had to come from their savings. To add to their pain, mortgage interest rates increased, which meant they had to use more of their available cash to cover the extra costs.

This meant they quickly spent their savings. That then put them in the unexpected (and unwelcome) position of having to spend much of their budget on fixed costs, AKA the boring stuff. They had little left over for the fun stuff they enjoyed the most.

As time went by, they found it more and more difficult to work within their restricted budget. With all the hard work they'd done to get them to where they were today, and the effort they'd put in to further their careers and grow their income, they felt entitled to have more of the things they enjoyed.

So they started making bad decisions. They didn't stick to the spending plan that made their budget balance. And because their savings were now gone, that spending went onto their credit card.

Over time, their credit card balance ballooned, which put even *more* pressure on their budget. Now, on top of their other spending, Riley and Eve also needed to cover their credit card payments. Their situation was growing increasingly impossible.

This continued for just under a year before they realised they were really stuck and couldn't see a way out. Eve told me later that this was one of the most stressful times in her life, and that it had almost ended her marriage. They loved their property, but realised holding onto it was unsustainable. So, after owning it for almost four years, they sold it.

Now, there *is* a silver lining here. Riley and Eve's property was a great investment. It was in a good area, and prices in their market had increased over that time. So the property's value had increased by just over $100k since they purchased it. And when they eventually sold it, after paying all the associated fees, they had enough money to pay off their credit card and be left with around $20k in change.

Not the end of the world, right?

Somewhat wiser, Riley and Eve returned to the rental market, happy to have their credit cards paid off and to return to a more comfortable budget position.

You can't fully eliminate risk, but you can manage it. To manage it well, though, you need to completely understand the risks you face. Riley and Eve weren't clear on the risks they faced, so they couldn't effectively manage them.

You can't fully eliminate risk, but you can manage it.

The main risk for Riley and Eve was lifestyle risk, which comes from making financial decisions or setting up strategies that stop you from making lifestyle choices that are important to you. Being forced into a position where you can't have the things you want isn't sustainable for any real length of time. Something will eventually give.

This forces you to change your strategy on the run, which leads to sacrifices or momentum-killing setbacks. Think through the things you do know about your situation now and how you want it to progress into the future. This will allow you to be smarter when you plan your money strategy and avoid these sorts of mistakes.

Early on in your money journey, lifestyle risk is one of the biggest risks you face. It's also the most overlooked one. Most people don't think through the impact of this risk or take the time to put a smart strategy in place to reduce it.

Building money momentum is like pushing a car. If you've ever had car trouble, you'll know that getting the car moving from a standing start requires the most effort. Once the car gets moving, it becomes easier to build up speed because you've got some initial traction.

You'll have to fight hardest for the first $10k, $100k, or $1m you save or earn through an investment. And that first amount will also take you the longest to get. But once you've created this foundation, getting to the next step will be easier because you already have a solid base of money working for you.

Remember our example of saving $10 every day/$3650 each year from Chapter 3? Assuming the same return as the overall Australian share market's long-term average (8.6 per cent), it would take you just over 14 years to reach $100k.

But, if you already HAD $100k, saving the same amount every day with the same returns would take you just over six years to make your next $100k. That's the same amount in less than half the time. If you've got $200k, it only takes four years to make your next $100k. And with $300k, it takes less than three years. With $400k...well, you get the picture.

Pretty soon you're stacking dollar bills faster than you can count them, taking daily champagne showers, and blinding passers-by with your bling.

Because the initial momentum is the hardest to build, you need to do *everything* possible to avoid 'momentum-killers' that can slow down your progress.

I first met Riley and Eve about two years after they'd sold that property. They'd started saving again and wanted to get back into the property market—but they didn't want to repeat their past mistakes and run into trouble again. So we did things a little differently the second time around.

This time, we mapped out how their personal and money situation was likely to change over time, including expected changes to their income and expenses. We plotted out their lifestyle wants. We included an allowance for unexpected expenses and those other things that tend to just 'come up'. We also made sure their strategy allowed for interest rate increases, so they felt comfortable that rising mortgage interest rates wouldn't cause them the trouble it had with their last property.

Once again, we found a property that fit into their strategy. It wasn't the same one they'd had previously, but it was a good investment that they were happy with. They were again moving forward, and happy to be making progress. But I couldn't help wondering how much their mistake had cost them.

They purchased their second property eight years after they'd bought their first place, and around four years after they'd sold it. In that time, property values had increased significantly. Because Riley and Eve been out of the market for those last four years, they'd missed out on all the growth over that time.

Plus, they'd also been forced to pay all the costs involved in buying and then selling their previous place, which was just over $70k in total. On top of that, their previous home had increased in value by a further $250k since they'd sold it. This put the total cost of their initial failed investment at over $320k.

Now, $320k may not be enough money to make you Instafamous. But as the example above shows, building money momentum is the hardest part of money success. Riley and Eve had to go back to the start and work to get back to where they'd been previously. If they hadn't suffered this setback, they'd have been able to make that $320k work for them and generate more money for the rest of their lives.

To put this in perspective, Riley and Eve were only in their early 30s, so they still had roughly another 30 years until they reached retirement age. If they'd invested that $320k over this time, it would have been worth over $3.8m (now THAT'S Instafamous levels of cash). That extra money could have allowed them to retire early, or on more income, or just to live like rock stars for a year flying first class around the world. I'm pretty sure they'd have liked to have had these options.

But maybe even more important for Riley and Eve were the non-financial costs. As I mentioned earlier, that period was one of the worst in their lives. They were constantly stressed, arguing all the time, and for more than two years they'd had that feeling of dread that comes from knowing you're slowly going backwards.

And they're not alone in the severe consequences of their mistake. I've met countless others who've faced this same pain (not always to the same degree, granted) because they didn't effectively manage lifestyle risk. I think every person should be able to live well without being limited by money, so I see this as a complete disaster.

The unfortunate thing is that it was all totally avoidable.

Starting any money strategy without thinking ahead is like walking blind.

Riley and Eve made the big mistake of not thinking ahead to manage their lifestyle risk. Going down any path or starting any money strategy without thinking ahead is like walking blind. You could be headed toward outcomes you don't want, haven't anticipated, and won't be happy to accept.

If Riley and Eve had taken the time to think through their strategy and map out where they were headed *before* they'd purchased their first property, they'd have realised that something wasn't adding up. They'd have seen that the path they were going down was heading to a place they wouldn't like. They'd also have seen that their financial goal of buying that particular property was unrealistic, and would have a lifestyle impact they weren't prepared to accept.

So do you think they'd have done things differently?

You *bet* they would have. When I worked with them to set up the plan for their second property, they mentioned several times that they wished they'd gone through this process the first time around. They were certain it would have helped them to avoid the problems they'd experienced, and allowed them to see how their situation would play out. It would have given them options.

If Riley and Eve had set up a solid plan for their first property, they could have chosen to either:

- buy a property at a lower price
- buy a property as an investment instead of for their own home
- make a small reduction to their lifestyle spending earlier
- save more money before they chose to have children and reduce Eve's income
- delay the property purchase until they were in a more comfortable position.

The planning process wouldn't have changed the options they had available: it's not magic. You can't flick a switch and immediately become able to plan a superyacht, a private jet, or the ability to tell your boss to stick it and then quit your job tomorrow with enough money to travel the world.

So for Riley and Eve, the process wouldn't have made their first property purchase possible with the time off work *and* the lifestyle spending they wanted. Something would still have needed to change. But if they'd been aware of the implications of their decisions, they could have made an informed choice about the best thing to do at the time.

I don't know which option they'd have chosen, but I do know they wouldn't have chosen the same path they did.

Like Riley and Eve, you'll find that effectively managing your lifestyle risk will move you a long way towards ensuring your choices work out for you the way you expect. When you do this, you need to consider a number of moving parts. At its core, though, the process is relatively simple. Manage your lifestyle by running through the steps below:

- Think about your income situation now, and any possible upcoming changes to it.
- Think about your expenses, and how these might change in the future.
- Think about the lifestyle expenses that are important to you, e.g. travel, experiences, renovations, etc.
- Think about what else in your situation could change, e.g. interest rates.
- Provide for the unexpected.
- Give yourself an emergency buffer or safety cushion.

These steps will help you plan to cover both your situation today and the way things might change over time. It will overlay any money choices on top of your situation so you can ensure everything fits together in a way you're comfortable with.

Pro Tip

The right amount to have in your emergency fund is different for everyone, depending on your employment and personal situation. But as a rough rule of thumb, three months of total living expenses is a good starting point. This number can exclude regular savings, investments or discretionary costs like travel.

PUTTING IT ALL TOGETHER

Getting a strategy in place is key to not letting the unexpected slow you down. It's also an important tool to help you avoid the inaction that comes from fear of the unknown. If your strategy covers the key risks that might impact your ability to get your planned results, you'll not only have a better foundation for those results, but you'll also have the confidence to take action.

Take the time to understand the things you should know about your situation and how it will change over time. Start by 'knowing your knowns'. This will help you avoid nasty surprises that can cause you trouble. Next, identify your 'unknowns'. Take the time to educate yourself and build knowledge around these areas. This will empower you to take the action you need at the right time, and help you build your money momentum faster.

Significant changes in your money strategy include things like big investments (e.g. buying property) or other choices that will have a long-term impact on your money position. When you make these changes, invest time (and potentially money) in revising your current strategy and setting up a solid plan. Make that investment now, and you'll enjoy the benefits into the future. Don't cut corners or follow the good old Aussie 'she'll be right' approach. Doing this could cost you, so keep your eyes open and know where you're headed.

The planning process will help you to identify any potential issues or roadblocks. You'll be able to understand your available options and their impact so you can prioritise what's most important to you. This will also allow you to adjust your strategy before you get started, which is always the best time to make changes.

The planning process isn't magic and won't make *anything* possible, but it will help you to manage risk, and give you the confidence you need to take action.

CHAPTER 7

Saving sucks

I get it.

Saving money sucks. It's hard, the rewards seem a long way away, and there's always something you want to spend your hard-earned cash on today.

Spending money is *way* more fun.

But something has to give. You can't just spend like a rock star without thinking ahead, or you'll create a life for your future self you won't enjoy.

Being successful with money often means saying 'no' to things that bring you short-term pleasure in the interests of getting things that bring you true happiness and fulfilment.

For example, it might mean saying 'no' to dinner with your mates or to that new tech toy. Or what about that AWESOME automatic mani-pedi machine on eBay? You know. The one with the fully adjustable controls and the 34 762 different colour settings that gives you a hand massage with your mani and a toe tickle with your pedi. It can probably even walk your dog.

It's often tough to say 'no' to this sort of stuff. But context can help to make saying it as painless as possible.

That context comes from goals and targets. They help you to focus on the long-term benefits of saying 'no'. In fact, when you're clear on your goals, you don't really say 'no' to something. Instead, you just say, 'I'd rather have this other thing I really want more.'

In this chapter, I want to help you understand how goals are absolutely necessary to be successful with money. I want you to see how they give you focus and keep you on track. I also want you to be clear on how to set them, and how to get started.

Goal setting is an often-overlooked area of money strategy; but in my view, it's one of the most important. That's particularly true when you're young and just getting started on your money journey.

Goals give you something to aim for

Imagine you're an archer who's competing in the Olympics, and it's the final gold medal round. You've prepared yourself. You've done your practice. You can almost *taste* victory.

You load your arrow, draw your bow, and set your breathing to take the shot that will lead you to victory and make you an immortal legend. You raise your bow, close an eye, look down the field to line up your shot … and … nothing.

You look hard, but can't see anything. Just a clear field. No indication of where to aim. No target. Nothing.

How likely do you think winning that gold medal is?

It's the same with money. Without a clear target to aim for, you'll never end up where you want to be. And even if you did, you wouldn't know you were there.

Without clear targets, you're like a tourist in a new city with no smartphone, map or Lonely Planet guide book to get you wherever you're going. You won't know where to head, so you just amble around the streets aimlessly. Then you get sidetracked down winding laneways, and end up wasting a bunch of your valuable time.

Sure you'll probably have some fun along the way, but you'll likely miss out on seeing the sights you *really* wanted to check out.

Plus, because you haven't plotted a course to get you where you're going, it's harder to avoid the troubled neighbourhoods. That means you run the risk of getting mugged (or at least having a hairy experience).

Again, it's the same with money. Without clear goals, you're much more likely to get sidetracked and take actions that actually move you AWAY from the things you want. That means more frustration, hard work and risks. And you might not even end up at a destination you're happy with.

Without a goal or target to work towards, you'll have no idea how you're progressing. You might see your savings or investment balance increasing, your debt going down, your income going up, or any number of other variables. But without clear targets, you'll never know whether what you're doing is enough.

You won't know whether you're saving enough. You won't know if you're investing enough. You won't know whether your investments are performing the way you need them to. And that will create constant doubts in your mind that will mean an element of money stress is always with you.

Without a goal or target to work towards, you'll have no idea how you're progressing.

This might sound ridiculously obvious. But I still find it surprising how many people don't have clear goals for their money. I've worked with over a thousand people now through one on one coaching and group training sessions. The number of those people who originally came to me with clear, well thought out goals is negligible. Many have broad goals or ideas and a general sense of where they want their money to head. Very few of them, however, followed through that extra half-step to get crystal clear on their targets.

Once you set your targets, you know where you want to end up and what you're working towards. This allows you to create a strategy to get there. And once you get that strategy in place, you can see how you're tracking over time to get to your target.

Then, as you review your progress, you can refine and improve your approach. But you need to have goals before you do anything else, because none of the other steps are possible without them.

I can say with *absolute* certainty that you won't just magically end up where you want to be without first getting clear on where that place is. Set clear goals so you can focus on where you're headed, get started on your action plan to get there, and reduce money-related stress along the way.

That said, it's important to realise that clear goals don't need to be rigid. In fact, the path to successful goal setting requires goals that evolve over time. As you get more refined with your approach (which I'll cover later in this chapter), you can also refine your goal. Meanwhile, having a clear goal in your sights will keep you focused and motivated.

Goal setting gives motivation

Another benefit of setting goals is that it allows you to reframe your thinking to make it easier to stay motivated when you're saving or investing. Like we said earlier, spending money is way more fun than saving it. But to save well, you *need* to give up some short-term pleasure for your longer-term benefit.

Clear goals give this sacrifice a purpose. Just 'saving' is way harder than saving for…

- that super-awesome new car you want…or
- that tech toy you've had your eye on for a while…or
- that home you really want on the beach with the sweet outdoor pizza oven and those fancy tap handles for your new kitchen that look oh-so-shiny in the morning sunlight.

Working towards clear goals helps you to remember *why* you're sacrificing the immediate pleasure of going on an epic spending spree or a weekend deep-sea fishing trip away with the boys.

I've already told you the story of our young exec Lola in Chapter 1. You'll remember that she was smashing it at her job, but had some slightly (okay, not so slightly) out-of-control spending habits that had landed her in a bunch of debt. She was in a bit of a bind, and got huge benefits from automating her debt reduction, saving and spending. But this was all only possible because we took the time to set clear goals for her, which allowed her to reframe her thinking and focus on what was actually most important to her.

Lola's mindset change didn't happen overnight, but once she'd set the wheels in motion, she focused on following through and keeping her eye on the prize. And I'm happy to say that like with most things in her life, Lola excelled at this also.

Just over 12 months — and one pay rise plus a couple of bonuses — later, we'd cut Lola's debt significantly. She now looked forward to her weekly payday when her guilt-free spending account was topped up AND she got to see another big chunk of her debt disappearing forever.

Our innately human tendency is to focus on short-term satisfaction at the expense of the less urgent — but often more important — longer-term goals.

And until you combat this tendency, getting positive results will always be challenging.

To overcome this tendency, you need to rewire the way you think about your money management and how you spend. People who are successful with money (or anything else) know this secret. It's the reason Olympic athletes spend years in training, facing the hard slog and getting up while most people are happily snoozing the morning away. It's why the people who rise to the top professionally hustle while most people are binge-watching Netflix on the couch.

Anything worthwhile requires commitment, motivation and a passion to succeed. But to keep up the intensity and do the hard work, you need motivation. Working hard is, well, *hard*. The easy path is just to 'opt out' and instead do more things that are more enjoyable in the moment.

Of course, there's a reason for the hard work. Combined with the right direction, it leads to success and great results. But getting there means pushing through the grunt work. It requires you to focus — and not on the hardness of the work, or the struggle, or the fact that other people are doing way more fun things than you are. Instead, you need to focus on the results or outcomes you're working towards. You need to focus on the goals you really want to achieve.

It doesn't matter whether your goal is buying your first home, retiring at 40, or just funding your next big overseas adventure. Maintaining focus on *that* thing makes it really easy to say 'no' to anything that will slow down your progress. Because you're working toward something and you can see how each small step moves you closer to your desired outcome, the struggle is worth it.

When you're slaving away on your laptop or at the office over the weekend, you need to focus on the big project milestone you're striving for. You're not thinking about how your mates are at a party, eating your bestie's famous hot wings. You're not thinking about how they're drinking your other mate's even-more-famous sangria. And you're definitely not thinking about how that sangria is made just the way you like it with the good wine and the extra orange and that secret ingredient she just won't tell you about no matter how many times you ask.

Focusing on your milestone instead of what you're missing out on renews your motivation and helps you to keep pushing through. It makes the work and the sacrifice easier. It makes it all seem not only okay, but a great idea and the very best thing you could be doing at that moment in time.

Without that focus on the result you're striving for, motivation is hard to maintain. When you're motivated, it's easy to keep your focus. This positive cycle keeps you moving forward toward the things you really want. Without focus and motivation, it's too easy to get distracted, tap out on your project, and instead run toward the sangria bowl with your red cup held high into the air.

Without that focus on the result you're striving for, motivation is hard to maintain.

I'd like to think it was my great advice and support that got Lola out of debt. And sure, we might have had a few tough conversations where I gave her a gentle (or not so gentle) push when she needed it. But in reality, she did most of the hard work herself.

Her progress wouldn't have been possible if she hadn't changed her approach to thinking about money. It also wouldn't have been possible without setting clear goals to drive her motivation, then maintaining her focus on those goals while she pushed through the difficult times.

The motivational power of goal setting shouldn't be underestimated. When you set up your money plan, bake your goals into it, then focus on those goals to keep pushing yourself forward. Think about how the steps you're taking today are moving you closer toward the things you really want. Don't lose sight of those things. Obsess about them. Dream about them.

Do this and you'll have a huge advantage over most others who ignore goal setting and then wonder why success with money (and everything else in life) is such a struggle.

What makes goals good

Just having a goal is not enough. I could set a goal to have five Lamborghinis, two Bugattis, a mansion, a helicopter, and a six-pack by next month. But there's a problem with the goals I've set (and not just my trashy taste). Setting a goal is not a silver bullet that magically brings you everything you want.

> **Setting a goal is not a silver bullet that magically brings you everything you want.**

Your goal needs to be good. It needs to be smart. But what actually makes a goal 'good'?

Much research has been done on goal setting. Unfortunately, a great deal of that research—referenced on sites like Forbes and Inc.com—shows that many goals that are set are never achieved. One study (referred to on both sites) showed that only 8 per cent of people who set New Year's resolution goals for themselves ever actually achieved them. This means 92 per cent of goal setters failed.

So what can you do to become part of the 8 per cent who actually achieve their goals?

The research identified four criteria for goal-setting success. When you're setting goals—whether they relate to money, career, personal life, or anything else—ensuring they meet these criteria will put you well on your way to hitting your targets and getting the things you really want.

Specific

Goals that work need to be specific, and the more specific the better. For example, don't just set a goal 'to get rich'. Instead, define what 'rich' means to you. You might say, 'I want to own my own home of a certain type in a certain suburb with a certain price tag. I want investments that give me an income of $100k each year. And I want an emergency fund of $50k for the unexpected.'

Being specific with your goals also involves setting a timeframe or deadline. Without this timeframe, your goals will just be an aimless exercise that you can continue to put off and get started on 'tomorrow'.

Plus, getting specific about your goals will help with all the other criteria below.

Pro Tip

Sometimes setting goals can be a circular process. For example, when you set your timeline, you may need to follow one or more of the other steps below and then return to your timeline to adjust it once you understand what's realistic.

Achievable

It's pretty obvious that if you set unrealistic goals, you won't be able to achieve them. So when you set your goals, spend some time understanding what's possible by when, so you know whether your goals are realistic and achievable.

It's great to set challenging stretch targets: I actually love doing this for myself. But I've also found from experience that when your targets are too difficult to achieve, you can end up giving up completely if they don't immediately come together. That can lead to a result that's worse than if you'd had no goals to begin with.

Stretching yourself is great, but ensure your goals will be achievable.

Actionable

Goals that work also need to be actionable. That means you need to be able to break them down into a process, or at least a series of steps or tasks.

A good goal should naturally suggest a starting point—something you can do first to get started. Important goals will usually involve several steps, each of which depends on the previous one.

Breaking down your goals into these individual tasks or steps is absolutely critical to being able to achieve them. If you don't know all the steps required to get to your goals, do more research or find an expert who can help you understand what's required. This helps to set your action timeline and gets you clear on the steps involved, and what to do next to make your goals a reality.

Accountable

The final step to setting good goals is to ensure you're accountable. You can do this in several ways:

- Post to your socials and ask your mates to hold you to your goals.
- Get an accountability buddy (partner, friend or family member), set goals together and then push each other to achieve them.
- Hire a professional coach, e.g. a money coach, financial adviser, business coach, life coach, etc.

If you set a goal without telling anyone, it becomes really easy to give up. After all, nobody will know except you—there are no consequences for failure. That may be why studies referenced on Inc.com and FastCompany have all shown that an accountability loop increases your chances of success.

I constantly experience this in practice with my own coaches for different areas of my business and life. Keeping yourself accountable brings your goals into focus every time you have your accountability sessions, and pushes you to take action.

Once you have goals, you can build an action plan

When we first met, Damon and Angela (not their real names) were doing okay with money. They were getting ahead, but were frustrated because their money and lifestyle targets seemed so big and far away. This frustration led to them make some poor money choices around spending that slowed down their progress.

They really wanted to buy their dream home: a three-bedroom place they could raise a family in that wasn't too far from the city in Sydney. If you know the Sydney property market, you'll know they weren't going to be able to get this cheap. Because this seemed like such a huge goal, they were overwhelmed. They didn't know how to get started, and it all seemed so far away. So, not surprisingly, they'd run into a patch of inertia.

This sort of inertia is common when a goal seems huge and you don't have a plan to get there. But once I showed Damon and Angela their options and the different paths they could take to get what they wanted, they settled on the strategy they were most comfortable with.

Once they'd done this, they were stoked: they could see what they needed to do to get their dream home, and had a clear timeline for it. They were actually surprised to find their goal was achievable in a much shorter timeframe than they were expecting.

Their plan involved buying an investment property as a stepping stone to get into the property market, then building an investment portfolio to grow alongside that property as a deposit for their dream home.

Setting that initial goal and then breaking it down into action steps allowed them to set clear short-term targets so they knew what to do next and where they needed to be to remain on track with their plan. It required some hard work and discipline, but the shorter timeline was highly motivating for them.

As soon as they had their plan, Damon and Angela felt much more confident. They've since been smashing their targets, and now are well ahead of the timeline we set for their plan. They're happy with their strategy and can now get on with the things they really enjoy, knowing they're on track to get what they want. But all this was only possible because they set a clear goal and broke it down.

When you first start building your savings, investments and assets for the future, your goals can seem so huge that they're almost impossible. They can make you nervous—as nervous as asking that special someone out on a date, while dreaming of moving in together...before the first date's even happened. You know the end result is theoretically achievable, but can't see how to get from your stammering, nervous mess to the magical moving-in day. That's okay. Worthwhile goals *should* make you nervous. Just don't let the fact you're nervous lead you to think your goals aren't realistically achievable.

It's also common to get frustrated when your goals are too difficult. You think it's all too hard, so you give up without even trying—or put off taking action until a tomorrow that never comes. And of course, this inaction makes you miss the opportunity to start making progress. Breaking your goal down into steps helps to make it feel way less difficult...which makes it easier to get started.

So dream big. Set outrageous goals. But make sure they meet the criteria for good goals as discussed above. Then take the extra step of breaking them down into the steps you need to take to get there.

Practical steps for money goal setting

I hope, by now, that you appreciate goal setting for the true wonder it is. I hope you can see how it gives you the context you need to go after the things that are important to you, and how it will motivate you. I also hope you understand how to set good goals, and why it's so important to go one step further and break your big goals down into actions.

But there's one more thing you need to understand to be able to effectively set goals.

I've met a bunch of people who get really stuck on goal setting. They say things like, 'I'm not sure what I really, truly want.' Or, 'I think I want this thing, but maybe I really want that one … and perhaps my future self will want this other one … should I go after them all?' Or even, 'I'd like this thing, but I don't know whether it's possible or what I need to do to get there and what comes next, and ARRGHHHHH, ITS ALL TOO HARD SO I'M JUST GOING TO SIT IN MY NEW MASSAGE CHAIR AND PLAY XBOX AND EAT SIX-DOLLAR CRACKERS BY THE FISTFUL!'

You can run into roadblocks setting goals if you think you need to know exactly what you want at the very start. The reality is that you don't. Unless you're an expert on personal finances, it's almost impossible to know which goals are realistic, which will put you in the best position, and which you should set for yourself. The reason is that you need to understand what's possible first. What most people don't get is that money goal setting is a process, not a single action.

The goal setting process involves four separate steps:

1. Set your initial goals.
2. Do a reality check and see whether they're possible.

3. Go back to your initial goals, then refine and clarify them.

4. Break down your new goals into actionable steps.

Take note: For Step 2, you'll need to dive into the numbers. And for both Steps 2 and 4, you'll likely need some financial expertise, research or outsourcing to help you understand your available options and which ones you can build into your action plan.

Each step is critical, so I don't want you to think you can skip any of the others, but Step 2 is probably the most important because it's the most involved. Once you have an idea of what you want, you need to see how it will play out in reality. That means looking ahead and confirming whether what you want is achievable in the timeframe you want.

If you're like most people (including me), not everything you want will be realistically achievable in your ideal timeframe. This is completely normal, so don't let it stop you. It's actually a win, because it tells you some adjustment is needed. If everything doesn't perfectly fit after your reality check, that just means you need to change something. It might be your income, job, how much you spend or save, your overall strategy or how you invest your money, but *something* needs adjusting.

Another key element in Step 2 involves truly understanding your available options. It's not enough to just hear that buying an investment property is better than buying your own home, or that buying shares is a bad idea because your uncle lost a bunch of money investing in shares.

> **When you set an important goal, you need to understand all the options that can get you there.**

When you set an important goal, you need to understand all the options that can get you there. And I mean really understand them. That allows you to figure out what's on the table, and what tools you have at your disposal to get you to your goals. Don't exclude anything before you understand it, because it might just be the very best thing you could do.

It may also *not* be the best thing, and that's cool too. But a great path to your goals is one you're confident in. It's also one that won't need to change because you missed something, and one that allows you to sleep well each night as you work towards your goals. When you're choosing that path, you can't skimp on this step. You might need to do some research (refer back to Chapter 3 for research tips) or get an expert to help you get this step right.

Many people don't think ahead. They either take action without full knowledge or just plod along, thinking that what they want is achievable but without a plan or a realistic timeline to get there. Eventually, they get to the point where they realise something needs to change.

Remember that the best time to make any big change is now, because it allows you to make small changes that deliver powerful results over time. For example, if you know you needed an extra $10k two years from now, you just need to start saving $100 per week. Not so bad, right?

If you waited a year to decide you needed this money though, you'd have to save $200 per week. That's a little harder. And if you didn't realise you needed it until the month beforehand, you'd have to save $10k in a month. For most people, this would be impossible.

This is a simple example, but the same principle holds with all money choices. The sooner you start making changes, the smaller they can be to deliver the results you want. So think ahead and choose your course with open eyes so you can pick the outcomes you want AHEAD of time and ensure you aren't forced to make drastic sacrifices in the future.

Pro Tip

If you're like most people, you'll benefit from having someone like an adviser or coach to guide you through this process. They'll help you to follow the steps in the right order, push you when needed to keep things moving forward, and importantly make sure your numbers are solid to help you make the best possible decisions.

PUTTING IT ALL TOGETHER

When setting your goals, you don't need to know exactly what you want to get started. Like most money-related things, you just need to choose a goal as a starting point. You can then adjust it once you have more information.

Don't get caught up thinking everything needs to be perfect before you jump in. Your goal can be flexible, and the goal setting process will help you to refine and adjust your thinking as you move through it. The goal setting process is circular, and often involves referring back to previous steps, and refining and adjusting along the way. This also keeps your goal in your sights and front of mind.

Without solid goals and targets, you're effectively wandering aimlessly. That means you're highly unlikely to take the steps you need to get the things you want. When you harness the power of goal setting though, you benefit from being clear on what you're working towards. You know whether what you want is achievable, and when you can get there. This boosts your motivation and makes you more likely to stay on track.

Don't underestimate the power of goal setting to make getting what you want easier. Follow the steps above, set good goals, and then make them happen.

CHAPTER 8

———

WTF is financial advice?

When most people think about money, their first thought is usually that they need some good money-making investments or smart products. I promise you: this is *not* what you need. Well, I should say this isn't **ALL** you need.

As you should see by this stage of the book, when you understand and implement your structure, strategy and solutions, the result is a clear, easy-to-follow path from wherever you are today to the money and personal and lifestyle results you want. This then gives you complete confidence in your strategy and the direction you're taking with your money.

But most people don't recognise this is the outcome they're really looking for.

And they want something even deeper too ... it's the real objective for *every* single person I've helped: to create a life not limited by money.

To me, this is the measure of money success. Money doesn't solve all problems, but it does give you options. Without enough money, it's unlikely you'll be able to do all the things you want. I believe every person should be able to live the life they want, without money holding them back. I think it's something everyone deserves, and something anyone can achieve if they're prepared to commit.

So in this chapter, I want to outline the actions you'll need to take to achieve money success.

So what's stopping you?

As I've already mentioned in the Introduction, there are three common problems that stop people from getting great results with their money:

- Being overwhelmed by too many options and too much information.
- Not being able to effectively balance financial success and enjoy an epic lifestyle at the same time.
- Being time-poor and not wanting to waste precious spare time doing something they aren't good at and don't enjoy.

These three problems create a perfect storm that gets you 'stuck'. Now when I say 'stuck', I don't mean 'doing nothing'. I just mean that you're stuck doing the same thing you've been doing in the past.

This is the inaction trap that's so common with money. You miss out on the opportunity to get more out of your current situation. You don't take the action you need to take to get the results you want.

I've already shown the financial benefits that come from taking action a few times in this book, so you should understand how important it is to solve these problems and get started.

The problem is that it's often hard to know where to start. If you're like most of our clients, it's just too confusing and difficult, and you don't have the time to make this happen on your own.

Going it alone is hard

Making smart money choices often seems like it should be easy, but it's not. In reality, there are loads of considerations, moving parts and potential mistakes to avoid. Getting a good outcome from your money planning means being aware of all of these variables and making the right moves in each area. Otherwise, the result can be a disaster.

> **Making smart money choices often seems like it should be easy, but it's not.**

I'd love for this chapter to take you through the exact steps you need to follow to build out an epic money strategy. Unfortunately, I believe that it's almost impossible for most people to get the best results from their money by going it alone. (The exception to this is personal finance experts or a very limited number of people who've invested a bunch of time and attention into their own money management for 10 or more years.)

There's so much complexity, and so many options and considerations that if you try to go it alone, you'll likely struggle at best. At worst, you can make mistakes that take you years to recover from.

Professional help from a Financial Adviser can give you a massive advantage when it comes to setting up your money strategy the right way from the start. This sort of help can not only make your life easier, but also get you faster results as you create a life not limited by money.

So instead of talking about how YOU can set up a smart money strategy for yourself, I want to explain the benefits of getting help from a professional. I also want to tell you what to look for as you search for the right person.

The benefits of professional advice

Here I've outlined what I believe to be some of the benefits of seeking professional advice.

A solid framework to make smart choices

The way I see it, financial advice has one goal: to help you create that life we've talked about throughout this chapter—the one that's not limited by money. To get there, you need to understand that your personal or lifestyle elements are inescapably linked to the financial side of your life. Remember: the right financial decisions for you are always driven by the lifestyle outcomes you want now and in the future.

That means the key to a great money strategy is to make informed choices about the options that will work best for you based on the outcomes that are important to you. So one of the most important benefits an adviser can provide is helping you to deeply understand your options, so you can make the best informed choices for YOU.

An adviser can help you to understand the advantages and disadvantages of each option available to you, including:

- Helping you to understand how your choices will impact you over time.
- Educating you around options that you may not have considered but should have.
- Explaining the common mistakes and roadblocks that stop people from getting results, and showing you how to avoid them.

This will allow you to choose the right combination of strategies, investments and financial products for you. A great adviser will have a solid framework that guides you through this process and makes it easy for you to make the right choices with confidence.

Balancing money and personal goals

The key to finding the perfect balance between your money results and personal or lifestyle goals is being able to choose the things that are most important to you with open eyes. In other words, you need to be aware of the impact of your choices over time.

Sure it's great to have all the latest tech gear, modern conveniences, a weekend away every month, a super-nice house to live in, and epic overseas trips twice a year. But if it's also important for you to hit financial goals within a certain timeframe, you'll probably find these priorities conflict.

Part of the planning process involves looking ahead at the likely impacts of making any changes on your financial results. Financial planning (modelling) software can show you how your financial position will change over time.

For example, you can see how quickly your asset position will increase based on your current income, spending and saving (and how that position changes over time). Then you can look at making adjustments to your strategy, i.e. buying a property, investing in shares or super or saving more/ less, and see how each choice might change your position.

This planning process shows you how hard you'll need to push yourself to reach the position you want to be in. If you look at the numbers and realise you're ahead of where you wanted to be, you can 'take your foot off the pedal' and start spending more. If you're behind, you might realise you need to save or invest more.

In this situation, a good adviser will have the right tools and knowledge to give you 100 per cent confidence in your numbers, and your choices based on these numbers. This then gives you the confidence to take action and change your approach, knowing you're not missing anything.

Saving you time

We've talked about being time-poor in previous chapters. Nobody wants to waste the precious little free time they have 'spinning their wheels' without getting results. An adviser can give you the tools and knowledge you need to ensure you spend any time you invest in your money management effectively. Plus, you can also outsource a lot of your financial administration to an adviser, who can do all the paperwork and basics around setting up financial products, investment accounts, etc.

An adviser can also answer any questions you have, so you don't waste time in the Google void trying to figure the answer out alone. Additionally, they'll give you confidence that their answer is the right one so you can act on it.

This means that every minute you spend on your money management is spent efficiently. You don't waste time chasing shiny objects, or struggling to figure out answers.

Not only that, but a good adviser will also draw any issues in other areas of your financial life (like tax, property, legal issues, etc.) to your attention. Because they sit at the centre of your financial world, they're across all the different elements of your money strategy. They understand how everything fits together, which means they'll often be the first to identify any issues that you need to address in your broader money strategy.

Financial advisers can't (normally) help you set up a mortgage or draw up a will. But because they understand how these things work, they can make sure you're getting the right advice in these areas.

They can save you a lot of time and stress when you're dealing with other professionals (e.g. accountants, mortgage brokers, and lawyers) too.

They speak the same language as these professionals and can work with them to ensure you don't miss anything through miscommunication.

In all of these areas, your adviser can help to save you a bunch of time, confusion and stress, and get you better results.

Pushing you forward

We've talked before about how easy it is to get caught up in day-to-day tasks and neglect important-but-not-urgent things like money management. Working with a proactive adviser will keep you focused and accountable to take the steps and actions you need to get the results you want.

A good adviser will also push you to update your strategy as your situation and what's important to you changes over time. This hugely underestimated benefit can make an ENORMOUS difference to how quickly you build momentum with your money.

Giving you confidence

Finally, a good adviser will give you confidence that everything related to your money is being looked after. You'll know your strategy is based on a robust framework and solid financials. You'll know everything related to your investments and financial products is being managed effectively in the background. Your adviser will be able to educate you on any issues you need to be aware of, so you feel comfortable with the actions you're taking. And you'll feel confident that they'll proactively bring anything that will get you better outcomes to your attention.

The ultimate result of having a good adviser is totally eliminating stress or concern around your money. You'll trust in your strategy, feel confident about your direction, and know you're on track to get the results you've planned for.

Roadblocks to getting good financial advice

Many people fail to get the money results they want due to roadblocks: misinformation and barriers that keep them from taking action. I want to cover a few of the most common roadblocks that can hold you back, so you can understand and avoid them.

Pro Tip

Many people believe they need to have a big savings or investment account balance to be 'right' for financial advice. This couldn't be further from the truth. Yes, traditional firms like the one I originally worked for may turn young people away, telling them to come back when they have at least $100k to invest. But now I work with people who have little or no savings and help them build that same $100k.

In reality, pretty much *everyone* can benefit from financial advice from the right adviser. Don't let thinking you're not ready be a roadblock to getting on the fast-track to money progress.

Cost vs benefits of advice

Financial advice costs money. Bad advice is cheap, but will cost you much more than the price you pay. Good advice is more expensive, but will benefit you far beyond the price you pay for it.

I've already mentioned how my financial planning business helps people to save more than seven times the national average, resulting in over $3.4m for the average 30-year-old by age 60. Now let me ask you, what would you pay for advice that would deliver you more than $3.4m over

30 years? Hint: the answer should be any number less than $3.4m (well not quite, but you get the point...)

The great news is that good financial advice will cost you much less than this. Recent figures show that for high quality advice, you'll pay around $5k-$10k per year. Even at the top end of this range—$10k each year—you'd only pay $300k over 30 years. That's $300k to have someone making sure you take advantage of every possible opportunity available. Someone who helps you make the right moves to hit the money and personal targets that are important to you. Someone who might save you $3.4m AND a bunch of time and stress along the way.

Is paying $300k for that $3.4m worth it?

Okay, so I'm being a bit cheeky now...but I included that question because it's a huge frustration for me. I talk to people all the time who are unhappy with the results they're getting. They're not making the progress with their money that they want (and *could* achieve). They're not living the lifestyle they want or deserve. They've often been 'stuck' in the inertia trap for years, and haven't taken any action to get out of it.

But these same people freak out at having to pay someone to get the advice, guidance, support and tools they need to get the results they want. They can see how having a good professional in their corner would help them achieve the money and personal results they want, but they just look at the cost and think it's too high.

I honestly can't understand this. I find it so frustrating, and not because the person I'm talking to isn't going to work with me. It frustrates me because I can see the results they could get and how much they want these results, but they choose to NOT take the action to achieve them just because getting help seems too expensive.

There are only three things in this world you can't put a price on: your physical health, your mental and emotional wellbeing, and your financial freedom and the lifestyle it provides. Personally, I'd pay anything to achieve my personal version of success in each of these areas.

Most people don't see it that way, though. I'm not saying that money is more important than any of the other two areas. Just like with the three money focusses (structure, strategy and solutions) all three are *absolutely* critical. You can't achieve total wellbeing/success without all of them.

But that means financial security IS necessary for total wellbeing. It will give you the foundation for your entire life. So don't skimp on the cost of a great financial adviser who understands you and can deliver you the things you want and need.

Now, that example above is based on the average results I get with *my* clients. Different advisers may get different results. But regardless, you should be able to see that a good adviser can make you way more than you'll pay for their advice.

Please don't let cost be a barrier between you and creating a life not limited by money. The benefits will be far more than the price you pay.

Pro Tip

Most people who don't have a good money strategy and support end up spending more than they would on the cost of a good Financial Adviser. The right support will likely save you far more than the fees you pay your adviser, so it's almost like you're getting the help you want and need for free.

Being time-poor

Getting smart with your money involves investing time in setting up a solid, comprehensive money strategy. And regardless of how time-poor you may be, being successful with money means *making* the time to make this happen. There will never be a better time than right now.

People often delay taking action with their money. They justify this by saying that they're waiting for some event or other distraction to be finished before they get their butt into gear and get started.

The problem with this approach is that the list of distractions and activities is never-ending. There will *always* be something competing for your time and attention. This is just life. It's easy to fall into the trap of constantly putting off getting your money sorted, waiting for that magical spell of downtime that never actually happens.

It may help to remind yourself that once you get your money sorted and on track, your ongoing time commitment is minimal. Once you get things rolling, you can get back to anything else you want or need to be involved in, knowing you're steadily heading towards the results you want.

Don't let 'not having the time' stop you from taking the action you need to get you the results you want.

Stop making excuses and just get started.

Being unclear on the results you'll achieve

This is really common, and—unlike the previous roadblocks—it's absolutely justified.

Especially if you've never used an adviser before, you'll have no idea of how everything will work. You won't completely understand the advice/planning process and what's involved at each step. You won't be able to see the results you'll achieve until you get to the end. And you probably won't know what your strategy will end up being.

It's impossible to understand all of these factors before you get started. Without detailed knowledge of financial advice or personal finances, you can't expect to understand every single element in comprehensive detail.

This means there's no way of knowing what your strategy will end up being or the benefits you'll actually get. When I start the planning process with new clients, I NEVER know what their strategies will end up being.

You can only know these things *after* you've explored all the options in detail and considered their financial and non-financial impacts. That means you need to know how you feel about each option and then talk it through to find the perfect strategy for you.

Pro Tip

While you won't know the exact final outcome or strategy you'll get from the financial advice process in advance, speak to your adviser before you jump in about some of the benefits you'll get. Also make sure they have a great process and the right tools to help you—you'll find specifics of what to look for in the next section.

The right adviser will offer benefits in so many areas that you didn't consider before you started the advice process. Setting up a good plan and keeping on top of it will net you hundreds of thousands—maybe even millions—of dollars over the long-term.

That means you don't need to know what your exact results will be: you just need to know they'll be good.

How to choose a great adviser

Getting a good adviser is absolutely critical to the success or failure of your money strategy, so you need to get this right. Almost every adviser and advice business works differently and advises in different areas, so it can be tricky to find the right one for you.

The good news is that there are key characteristics to look out for to help you get the right results from your financial adviser. I'll step you through these characteristics in detail below, so you know what to look for as you choose your adviser.

They have a robust planning process

As I mentioned above, there's no one method of delivering financial advice. At a bare minimum though, your adviser should guide you through the following steps:

- Getting crystal clear on where you're at now and what's important to you when it comes to money.
- Understanding what might change over time.
- Understanding the options or scenarios you're thinking of including in your strategy, and suggesting options you may not have considered.
- Helping you to understand the financial impact of the options identified above.
- Educating you around these options (including the benefits and risks of each) so you can choose the right option/s from an informed perspective.
- Recommending a combination of strategies to help you get what you want—i.e. a plan.
- Outlining clear action steps to make that plan happen.
- Setting up any solutions (products, investments or structures) to support your strategy.

The steps above will help you set up a plan for your money and the products, structures, and investments that support it. But I've found that most people get a heap of benefit from working with an adviser after setting up their plan to make sure they **get the results they planned for** over time. If this is important to you, your adviser should also:

- have a structure process to keep you on track
- adjust your strategy as your situation and objectives change.

When you're talking to an adviser, ask them how their process works to confirm they're ticking off the points above. If any seem to be missing or light on detail, keep asking more questions until you understand exactly how their process works.

They work with people like you

Nobody wants to be a square peg in a round hole. An adviser who works with clients like you every day will be more across what's most important to you. They'll also know the common tips and traps to look out for.

Your needs will be different depending on whether you're a young professional, about to retire, an expat or a business owner. And it's almost impossible for one adviser or business to be across all the important issues for every person in every situation.

Find an adviser who works with people like you, who are at the same life stage, and who have the same work situation and goals. This way you'll have confidence that they deeply understand the common challenges, frustrations and mistakes, and how to overcome or avoid them.

They help you understand the 'why'

If you only understand the 'what' of your money choices (i.e. which strategies, investments and products to choose), without knowing the 'why' (i.e. how each one works, and the benefits and risks), you'll always lack confidence in your strategy and the direction you're taking.

Building your knowledge is one of the pillars of creating true confidence in your money plan. Ask your potential adviser how they'll educate you as part of their process.

Money strategies always involve some form of trade-offs. A good adviser will help you to understand the benefits and downsides of any choice, so you can make an informed decision about what you're most comfortable with.

They should also help you to understand the most relevant alternative courses of action so you can see why you're NOT choosing them. This will give you even more confidence in the strategy you decide to follow.

Pro Tip

Occasionally you might need specific advice on an issue relating to your finances. For example, you might want to invest some money, choose the right super fund, or set up income replacement insurance.

This sort of specific advice will generally NOT create a life not limited by money—or most of the other benefits outlined in this chapter either. For these benefits, you'll need 'comprehensive advice'.

Specific advice and comprehensive advice are two very complex areas. I don't have space to cover the difference between them in this book, but for more information, check out the article I wrote at bit.ly/getunstuck-advice.

Understand the sort of advice you want before you get started so you can find the right adviser for you.

They manage conflicts of interest

(Apologies in advance to all my Financial Adviser mates who read this section. I know you won't like what I say below. But here goes ...)

Having complete confidence in your money strategy is ABSOLUTELY CRITICAL for you to take action and follow your strategy over time. So you need to avoid anything that takes away from your confidence levels. And the way your Financial Adviser is paid can have a *huge* impact on those confidence levels. That's why I'm a bit opinionated when it comes to how your adviser charges.

The vast majority of Australian Financial Advisers receive payments that cause a conflict in their advice process. The most common payments, and those that have the biggest impact, are:

1. Sales commissions.
2. Asset-based fees.
3. Referral fees.

Let's look at each of these in detail.

1. Sales commissions

Sales commissions are payments made when an adviser sells a particular financial product—for example, income replacement, disability and life insurance. The problem with these commissions is that they can reduce your confidence in the advice you're receiving. Your adviser is getting paid a commission, which causes doubt around whether they've recommended a particular product because it's genuinely the best one for you, or because they'll get paid when you buy it.

Before I started my own financial advice business, I was an employee at another company that accepted commissions. I was against this, but didn't have the power to force them to change how they charged fees.

Now, I'm a big believer in income replacement insurance for young people, and I also think life insurance is really important for couples and families. I believe both types of insurance provide a solid foundation for your money strategy. But in my old job, whenever I recommended that clients set up cover and they found out I was getting paid commission, they'd (rightly) question my advice.

Was I recommending this insurance cover because I REALLY thought it was important? Or was it because I'd get paid thousands of dollars if they said yes?

I was only recommending the level of insurance my clients needed to protect them against the risks they wanted to cover, but they were right to ask the question. And that question reduced their confidence in my advice, which was disastrous. It meant they were less likely to take the action they needed to, and more likely to give up on the strategy. And I saw significantly more clients cancelling their insurance cover over time as a result.

Since starting my financial advice business, I've made it clear that I don't accept commission payments on any new insurance products I help my clients set up. And my approach to providing financial advice on insurance is exactly the same now as it was when I was an employee at my previous company.

The other benefit of getting insurance advice with no commission is that you pay roughly two-thirds of the cost for EXACTLY the same cover. Because the insurer doesn't have to pay that commission to an adviser, they can charge you less.

So if you're setting up long-term insurance cover (as most young people do), you could save tens of thousands of dollars over the time period you hold your cover. These financial benefits are (almost) as valuable as the increased confidence.

That's why I strongly recommend looking for an adviser who doesn't accept commission payments: you'll be more confident in their advice and save a bunch of cash over time.

Look for an adviser who doesn't accept commission payments: you'll be more confident in their advice and save a bunch of cash over time.

2. Asset-based fees

Asset-based fees are another common form of conflicted payments. These are fees where your adviser is paid more for managing more money for you through financial products like super funds and investment accounts.

Most Financial Advisers charge fees for asset management in this way— usually around 1 per cent of the value of the investments they're managing. So if your adviser manages $100k of your money, they'll charge you $1k each year. If they manage $200k, they'd charge you $2k each year, etc.

The problem with this approach is that it can cause a conflict around helping you choose your options. Say, for example, you were considering either buying property or investing your savings somewhere else. An adviser who charged asset-based fees would be paid more if you invested the money rather than buying property.

Look for an adviser with a fixed fee structure. That way you know they have no incentive to push you down one path over another.

When you're making big decisions like this, you want to know the person advising you has no interest other than helping you make the best possible decision. In my opinion, you can't know this if that person receives asset-based fees.

So look for an adviser with a fixed fee structure. That way, you know they have no incentive to push you down one path over another.

3. Referral payments

The final form that potentially conflicted fees come in is referral payments. This is where your Financial Adviser is paid a fee by another company for referring you to them. This is common with other financial professionals like mortgage brokers, accountants and property spruikers (the people that sell you off-the-plan properties).

If your adviser is paid in this way, they become conflicted because they only get paid if you accept the other professional's recommendations. This means they're likely to endorse the other person's advice, which will often lead you to doubt the advice you're receiving.

Before you engage an adviser, ask them whether they have any third-party referral payment arrangements so you can make an informed choice about whether this might impact the advice you receive.

Before you engage an adviser, ask them whether they have any third-party referral payment arrangements so you can make an informed choice about whether this might impact the advice you receive.

The alternative: Fee Only advice

The alternative to these conflicted payments is a 'Fee Only' model, where your adviser quotes you a fixed, dollar-based fee for the help you want. For example, based on what you need, your adviser might say the cost will be $3k up front and $3k each year that you continue working together.

I've found this Fee Only model is best for building confidence in the advice you're receiving, and giving better financial outcomes. When you work with an adviser under a Fee Only basis, you know they have no financial interest or motivation other than making sure you're super-stoked with their advice so you tell all your mates.

It's worth repeating: if your adviser receives other payments or benefits like sales commissions or kickbacks, asset-based fees, or referral fees, it can cause you to doubt the advice you're receiving. This can reduce your confidence in your strategy, and ultimately lead you to give up on it without getting the results you're aiming for.

Added to this are the significant financial benefits I outlined above that can save you a bunch of money over time. Every dollar you save is another dollar you can put toward creating a life not limited by money.

So take the time to understand how your adviser is paid, and consider the potential impact this could have on the advice you are given and the financial results you'll get over time. BEFORE you engage anyone, ask them whether they have any third-party referral payment arrangements. This will allow you to make an informed choice before you start the process.

Your adviser should be very transparent about this: it's a legal requirement for them to disclose all this information.

They have a process with a result focus

Sometimes I get really excited about helping people to build their financial strategy and money plan. But I also recognise that it's not the plan that's important. Instead, it's the outcomes. The results you get are why you bother creating the plan in the first place. They're all-important.

I also know from experience that it's really hard (at least in the short-term) to get your planned money results without having someone in your corner to push you to make it happen. As I mentioned above, having a great Financial Adviser is a total game changer when it comes to pushing you to follow through on your plan and getting the results you expect.

There's another important reason to have someone with an outcome focus in your corner too. It's because your situation, what's important to you, and the general financial landscape is constantly changing. This means that if you want to continually get the most out of your situation, you need to update your strategy on an ongoing basis.

As a practical example, when I first started advising young people, I'd help them to set up their plan, and then schedule a catch-up meeting with them in 12 months to review their progress. Of course, a year is a long time, and I found that in EVERY SINGLE REVIEW, my client was at least slightly off track. They weren't in the position we'd planned for. Many weren't even close.

I'd ask them why and get treated to a never-ending list of situations and 'emergencies' (read: excuses). So, to reduce my clients' chances of getting off track, I tried shortening the review cycle to every six months. Then, when everyone still ended up off track, I tried every three months. Finally, I tried short, monthly phone check-ins, and found they got the best results. It's hard to get *too* off track in a month.

Now, I love my clients and enjoy our monthly chats. But if I could get the right results with fewer check-ins, I'd do it in a heartbeat. Even though our calls are only 20-40 minutes, I still invest a fair bit of time in this. So do my clients. But it just doesn't work any other way.

This is what I mean when I say you should look for a Financial Adviser with a solid ongoing process who'll ACTUALLY deliver your planned results.

Ask your adviser how their process is structured, and think through what this means for the likelihood of getting your planned results.

> **Ask your adviser how their process is structured, and think through what this means for the likelihood of getting your planned results.**

Pro Tip

High-touch advice like this will cost you more on an ongoing basis than an adviser who sets up a strategy and then sends you on your way, telling you they'll check in with you in a year. But you're much more likely to get the results you plan to achieve, so it's worth it.

PUTTING IT ALL TOGETHER

So many young professionals struggle on their own to figure out what sort of help is out there and which resources they can use to more easily get the money and lifestyle outcomes they want.

Don't make this mistake.

(continued)

If you're struggling without a framework to make smart money choices, or can't seem to balance your financial and personal/lifestyle progress or find the time to make money management happen, don't let it push you into the inertia trap.

Instead, take the time to educate yourself about your options. If you've made it this far, you're probably a step ahead of the curve. Understand what financial advice is, how it works, when you can benefit from it, how to find the right adviser for you, and how the process should work. That way, when the time is right for you, it's easy to take that first step. It can be a confusing area, but getting this right is the easiest way to break through inertia and move toward the results you want.

The good news is that if you've got plenty of time on your side, anything is possible—but only if you take action. The sooner you get a solid strategy in place, the easier it will be to hit your money targets and live well today, knowing you're setting yourself up to ALSO live well in the future.

The Financial Adviser you choose will have a big impact on your results, so it's important to make the right decision before jumping in. You should now understand how advice works and what to look for in an adviser.

I know that talking about money can be scary, especially if you haven't used an adviser before. But don't fear, you've got this. Any good adviser should make you feel 100 per cent comfortable, so don't be worried about just laying out where you're at when you're chatting to them.

Your adviser should be able to answer any possible questions you have. ANY possible questions. If something doesn't make sense or you have any concerns at all (or you simply want to know more about why something works the way it does), just ask.

Choose the right adviser, and you'll be supported the entire way through your journey to creating a life not limited by money. It takes some work to get there, but the results are worth it.

SECTION 3
SOLUTIONS

In the first two sections of this book, we covered structure and strategy. As a reminder, your structure is what helps you save more money. Your strategy is what makes your savings work harder to make you more money. Setting up good solutions is the final step, and the one that helps you grow your assets while you avoid setbacks and momentum-killing mistakes.

To be honest, I'm a big fan of alliteration, but by the time I got to third step in the 'Get Unstuck' journey, I was running out of 'S's. So I should clarify that when I talk about solutions, I mean the investments and product solutions that back up your money plan.

Solutions are the final element of a solid money strategy. When most people think about getting their money sorted, they start here. But this is completely backwards. Your investments and products should flow naturally from the plan or approach you want to take with your money.

If you know how to approach investing and what to look out for, it's really easy. But the psychology around investing pushes us all to take the wrong approach. And many suffer as a result.

So, in the next four chapters, I'll take you through the four most common (and most important) investment solutions you need to understand. These are:

- Cash.
- Shares (and share-type investments like managed funds).
- Property.
- Superannuation (retirement accounts).

These four investment solutions are the most common for a reason: they work.

They're tried and tested. They do what they're supposed to do. They turn money into more money.

Sure, you can invest in almond plantations, timber mills and crypto currency, but if you're smart with your strategy and structure you don't need to. The four investment solutions listed above can make you more than you need to create a life where money isn't a limiting factor.

But it's easy to get caught up in the hype and the myths around investing, and make bad choices. If you know the key questions to ask though, you can avoid all the common mistakes and shortcut your way to money success.

So, in this section, I'll take you through the key things you need to understand when you invest. That means this section of the book is the most technical, but bear with me.

CHAPTER 9

Death and taxes

Before we get into the investment solutions you can use to round out your structure and strategy, you need to be across a couple of really important things first. These are your tax and cash position, which feed through into all areas of your investment (and broader) strategy.

If you don't know the tax rules, you can miss opportunities to get ahead faster.

You might miss strategies that could cut your tax bill.

You could set up your investments ineffectively, and have to pay extra tax on your investment income or when you sell.

Or you could get pissed with the amount of tax you're paying every year, but have no idea what you could do better, leading you to frustration.

Regardless, you'll constantly wonder whether you should be doing something smarter with your money. This can cause you to doubt your strategy, get distracted and end up off track.

Cash sounds so simple. After all, it's just money: you kinda have it or you don't. You either have savings or you don't. You can either buy stuff like that super-epic cupboard organiser with the 53 adjustable pockets that comes in 14 colours … or you can't.

But there's more to cash than meets the eye.

Your cash position and cash savings are what allow you to invest with confidence. If you're not smart around your cash position, you can run into serious trouble when you invest. Like Riley and Eve in Chapter 6, you can get caught short and be forced to make sacrifices around your spending. And this can cause serious stress and angst.

I've outlined the key tax and cash issues you need to be across below. Get these areas wrong and you'll suffer through years of slow progress. You may also make mistakes that set you back and make you waste years getting back on track. Getting them right, on the other hand, will set the foundations of your money and investment strategy. You'll get the most out of your investments and keep more of your hard-earned cash.

Tax hacks to save you stacks

The average full-time worker in Australia pays $22218 in income tax to the government each year. But tax applies to more than just your employment income.

Whether you realise it or not, tax impacts every area of your money. You pay tax on the bank interest you earn on your savings. You also pay it when you sell investments, receive investment income or buy property. So if you want to make smart money choices, you need to think about the tax impact of your decisions.

To help you do this, I want to take you through some tax basics that will help you understand how to start getting smarter with your tax.

In Australia, we work on a marginal tax rate system, meaning you're taxed at a higher rate as your income increases. This system can be a little confusing, so I want to step you through it.

Here are the Australian tax brackets and rates:

Taxable income	Tax rate (including Medicare levy)
0 – $18 200	0%
$18 201 – $45 000	18%
$45 001 – $135 000	32%
$135 001 – $190 000	39%
$190 00+	47%

*Please note that the tax rates included in this table and the examples throughout the rest of this section and the book are based on the 1 July 2024 tax rate changes.

It's important to note here that the marginal tax rate *only* applies to the income within a particular bracket. For example, if your income is $90 000, you'd pay the following tax:

- $0 – $18 200 @ 0% = $0
- $18 201 – $45 000 @18% = $4824
- $45 001 – $90 000 @32% = $14 400
- **Total tax = $19 224**

The important thing to note here (which many people find confusing) is that when you go into the next income tax bracket, the higher tax rate only applies to income ABOVE that bracket's threshold.

Most people think moving into the next tax bracket will somehow mean they end up with less money in their bank account each month when they get paid. Not true: there's no point on the tax scale for ordinary taxpayers (excluding other benefits and HECS payments, etc.) where a higher income would mean you ended up with less money after tax.

So don't hit the panic button every time you get a pay bump that pushes you up a tax bracket . Instead, embrace it. You'll end up with more money in the bank after tax, so don't stress.

You only get one tax scale

Another thing many people find confusing is that in Australia, you only get one tax rate. This means the tax rate is exactly the same for your salary, the interest you earn on your savings account, and any investment or property income.

When individual taxpayers do their tax returns, the Australian Tax Office (ATO) doesn't really care about the source of any income (other than for a few uncommon exceptions, e.g. overseas or pension income). Instead, they simply add up your income from all sources and take away any deductions to calculate your overall 'assessable income'.

It's this assessable income figure that you pay tax on, based on the rate from the table above.

Tax impacts all investments

You pay tax on *every* dollar you generate through investing. This includes any interest you earn on your bank accounts, rental income from an investment property, or dividends from shares or other investments. When you do your tax return, you need to declare any income generated through investing, which then all adds to your taxable income.

As mentioned above, you only get one tax scale. So your investment income is added to your other income from employment or other sources, and the total income is taxed at your marginal rate. Unfortunately, there's no way to avoid this.

So when you look at an investment, think about your after-tax return. A high headline return figure on your investments means little if most of it's eaten away by tax. Often the tax you pay on your investments is hidden, because you receive the full return at one point, but don't pay the tax until the end of the year.

Whether you realise it or not though, you ARE paying tax on your investment income and returns. So understanding how the tax on your investments works before you get started lets you create a strategy to get the best tax outcome possible.

What you can do to (legally) cut your tax bill

With our high (and ever-increasing) tax bills, it's more important than ever to get tax-smart. You want to keep more of your hard earned cash and have more money to save, invest or just spend on smashed avo at your favourite brunch spot.

So the most important thing you can do to get smarter around tax is to educate yourself about the tax rules and how they impact your existing (and future) money choices.

I've briefly outlined what you can do to reduce your tax below. Not all of them will be right for everyone, but I wanted to cover them so you'd know what to look out for.

Know what you can claim

You should understand what you can claim based on your occupation. Most occupations these days have expenses that are deductible, particularly given our increasing tendency to work from home. If you don't know what you can claim, you're likely missing out on tax deductions.

If you're an employee, take the time to understand what you can claim based on your job and employment arrangements. If you don't know where to start, the ATO has lots of helpful content on their website. There are even some examples of things you can claim in different occupations.

Knowing exactly what you can claim at the start of the tax year means you can keep good records.

Most people don't start thinking about what they can claim until the tax year has ended. But by then it's too late. The best time to start your tax planning is on the first day of the tax year (1 July in Australia). Knowing exactly what you can claim at the start of the tax year means you can keep good records. This will then set you up to get the most deductions when you do your tax at the end of the year, while helping you to avoid trouble with the tax man.

Get a good tax adviser

The rules around tax are tricky, and can get really complex. Getting help—either from a good adviser who understands tax or a personal tax accountant—will normally pay for itself through the tax they save you. Someone who's in your corner and knows the rules can help to direct you to the things you should be thinking about, and cut through the confusion around tax.

As well as eliminating the confusion, this will also give you more confidence in your strategy. The right advice will help you to feel confident that you're doing everything to keep as much of your hard-earned income as possible.

A quick note on tax accounting. There's not much money in doing personal income tax returns for people in simple situations. If you're an employee who doesn't own multiple properties, a tax accountant can only charge you a few hundred dollars to do your tax return. Accountants go through years of training and pay all the costs that running a business entails. So to make any money doing your tax return, they have to spend as little time as possible on it.

Unfortunately, this normally translates to a level of service that's below what you'd ideally want from a tax adviser. This annoys me when I try to get good accounting help for my clients, but it's hard to avoid.

To get the most from your relationship with your accountant, you need to prepare for your meetings. Do some research or speak to your financial adviser/coach and prepare a list of questions you'd like your accountant to answer. Don't just tell them you want to reduce your tax. Instead, try to identify options that might help, and then ask specific questions about each one.

As a bonus, this will help you to build your knowledge around options that can help you cut your tax bill.

Tax-smart investing

Tax impacts every investment you make, which means that some investments are more tax-effective than others. So when you invest, you should understand what to look for to get the best tax result.

Australian shares—and the managed investment funds that invest in Australian shares—can be very tax-effective investment options, because some tax is already paid on any income (dividends) you receive from your shares. This gets a little technical so I won't go deep into the details, but look up 'imputation credits' if you want to find out more.

The short story is that Australian companies pay tax at the company tax rate of 30 per cent. Most big companies pay dividends on their shares after they've paid this tax at 30 per cent. So if you get income from those dividends, you'll receive a tax credit for the tax that's already been paid. When this happens, you only need to pay tax on the difference between your marginal tax rate (calculated as above) and the 30 per cent company tax rate.

Other investments like cash savings are very tax-ineffective because you're slugged with tax on the full amount of interest income you earn (more on this below).

Understand the tax impact of different types of investments so you can make smarter, more tax-effective investment choices. And do this *before* you invest: it can be difficult and expensive to restructure investments after you've pushed the 'go' button. I've seen many people fall into the trap of not structuring their investments correctly, and the extra tax they end up paying drags down the return they'd have otherwise received on the investment for years.

Borrow to invest

When you borrow money to invest, any interest payments you make on this debt are tax deductible.

Borrowing to invest in anything is called 'gearing' because it's like using the leverage of a gear to get more power behind your investment strategy. Gearing is seen most commonly when people borrow to buy an investment property, but the next most common scenario is borrowing to invest in shares. Be aware this strategy only works when the (after-tax) interest rate on your debt is less than the return you'll get on your investment (after tax and all investment costs).

If the after-tax cost (interest rate) on the money you borrow is less than the investment return, you make money. But of course, if the after-tax cost of your borrowing is higher than your return on investment, you end up behind.

There *are* tax benefits and deductions when you borrow to invest, but use this strategy to make money, not just to get tax deductions. I've seen a bunch of people get caught up in the tax advantages of an investment and overlook the actual return. Never invest for tax purposes alone: if an investment isn't good without the tax benefits, it's probably not good at all.

Never invest for tax purposes alone: if an investment isn't good without the tax benefits, it's probably not good at all.

The bottom line is that if you're considering borrowing to invest, look at the return you can realistically expect on your investments and make sure it's less than the costs you're going to pay.

If you ever borrow money to invest, do it with extreme caution. Borrowing to invest allows you to accelerate your returns, but it also amplifies losses. I've seen this strategy work well in practice, but I've also seen it unfold as a complete disaster.

To go down this path, you need a solid income ($100k+ as a minimum). You'll also want to map out a solid overall plan so you know the strategy fits with your other wants. Seriously consider getting good financial advice so you know all your bases are covered.

Make extra superannuation contributions

In Australia, superannuation (super) refers to the funds you save over your working life to provide for your retirement. These funds provide tax benefits, and are a really simple way to get extra tax deductions. The only downside is that once you've put money into your super fund, it's locked away until close to retirement when you can access it.

At the time of writing this book, you can contribute up to $30 000 each year to your super through 'concessional contributions'. This $30k limit includes the money employers pay into their employees' super, but it still leaves room for most people to make extra contributions and get an extra tax deduction. You can check out the ATO website for up-to-date limits on concessional contributions at www.ato.gov.au.

Extra super contributions can save you thousands of dollars in tax each year. They also allow you to grow your super faster. But because the money ends up locked away, it's probably not the first thing to do to get a tax deduction.

Most people want to first build their savings and grow some investments outside of their super, which isn't a bad idea. But once you've got some traction with your personal savings and investments, extra super contributions can be a great way to save tax and grow your super at the same time.

Start a business

When you're a regular (PAYG) employee, the things you can do to reduce your tax are limited. The tax rules in Australia are geared towards business—and small business in particular. This clearly isn't for everyone, but starting a business or side hustle can generate some extra income *and* give you more options to reduce your tax bill.

A note on tax structures

People often ask me whether they should use a trust or company structure to reduce their tax. This is a complex question, and the answer depends on your situation. In short, unless you have a very high income ($250k+) or significant investment assets, the costs normally outweigh the benefits.

When you run a trust or company structure, you'll need to pay an accountant every year to do the tax work and compliance for the tax entity. You'll also need to pay registration fees with the regulator. If you aren't generating a substantial amount of income through these tax structures or entities, you'll probably find the costs are greater than the tax you save.

That said, if you think this sort of structure is right for you, do some research or speak to a good adviser to get across the details.

Get tax-smart

We already pay lots of tax in Australia, and you don't want to pay more than you have to. So take the time to build your knowledge and get smarter with your tax planning. Learn what you can claim to maximise your deductions and tax refund. Explore the options in this chapter to understand what might work for you.

Getting your tax strategy right means you'll keep more of your income for your savings, your investments, or simply for fun. Tax can be the silent killer, but only if you allow it to be. The best time to get smarter with tax is today.

Sweet, sweet cash-ola

Next I want to change it up slightly and talk about cash savings. This ties in with your tax, and is one of the basics you need to be on top of before you jump into any sort of investing.

Cash is one of those things that gives you peace of mind. When you have it, you feel like you can do anything. Want to take off for the weekend? Done. Want to splash out on a fancy dinner at your favourite trendy restaurant? Done. Want to blow your cash on a bunch of stuff you think might make your life better but don't really need and will never use? Done too.

Without cash, you don't have the same peace of mind. You worry about being caught short if something comes up that you need money for. But having cash can also be a bad thing—particularly if you hold too much of it. I've outlined the key issues you need to be aware of around cash below.

Cash is king

We've all heard the saying 'cash is king'. And it couldn't be more true. Even when you want to invest to get your money working harder for you, cash is still absolutely necessary.

Yes, investing is critical if you want to avoid being forced to work forever, not to mention grow your assets and have a second income. But any sort of investing actually requires cash. Not just cash to invest, but leftover cash you can easily access when needed.

Even great investments will have periods where they go down in value.

We'll go into detail about investments over the next few chapters, but for now recognise that the value of most investments outside of cash will go up and down over time. Investment markets are unpredictable. You won't know when they'll go up, and when they'll go down. Even great investments will have periods where they go down in value. This is totally natural, and is based on the market cycle. But if you're smart about how you invest, this won't cause you any problems at all.

The only time you'll ever lose on good investments is when you sell. Even if you choose good investments, having to sell or exit them when investment markets are down WILL lose you money.

Pro Tip

To avoid losing money on your investments, you never want to be forced to sell or exit them at a time that will mean you lose money on them. This sounds simple, and it kinda is … but most people overlook it when they invest.

To avoid being forced to sell, you need to have enough money for all the other spending you want or need to do. As we talked about in Chapter 6, you need to cover all your day-to-day spending, plus any bigger ticket 'lifestyle' expenses. You should also provide for unexpected expenses. And there's one final thing you need to have money put aside for too. In Chapter 6, we introduced it as your 'emergency fund'—but I like to call it your 'security blanket'.

Think of this security blanket as your emergency expense money. So what's the difference between 'unexpected' and 'emergency' expenses? Unexpected expenses are larger costs that come up, and that you wouldn't plan for. For example, you might smash your phone and need a replacement, get an unexpected dentist bill, crash your car and need to pay an insurance excess, etc. These costs range from a few hundred to a couple of thousand dollars.

Emergency expenses, on the other hand, are things like leaving your job and needing to take a month out from the workforce while you find a new role. They could also involve large medical expenses, or a family emergency that requires money, etc. While you can count on some unexpected expenses popping up each year, emergency expenses are less frequent, and you really hope they never happen. Just in case, though, you still need money for them.

There's no hard rule for how much you need to provide for emergency expenses. The number is different for everyone, and is driven by where you're at now, how your situation could change over time, and how comfortable you feel with different levels of cash reserves. To get a sense of *your* number, ask yourself, 'If I only had $x in the bank, would I be comfortable that I wouldn't be caught short?'

You're not actually *going* to lock away the rest of your cash indefinitely, but the question will get you thinking about what emergencies might come up, and how much you'd need for each. Consider how likely each of these scenarios is, and how much you might need for it. This will help you to come up with your security blanket 'number'.

If you need a place to start, the figures I typically see are between three to six months of your living expenses. Of course, you'll need a good handle on how much you're spending to figure this out. If you haven't already, download our saving and spending planner [bit.ly/GUStools] to outline your spending. This will also give you a breakdown of your total spending on a monthly basis.

If you have a solid job in a highly employable role (i.e. it would be easy to switch jobs and find work quickly) and don't have many financial commitments or any dependants, you might be comfortable with a lower number. But you should still have *some* cash at hand to ride out any emergencies and give you peace of mind.

If you don't have much cash available right now, don't sweat it. You can build this up over time. I'm strongly against using credit cards as part of your day-to-day strategy, but they can be handy in an emergency. So if you don't have enough cash savings for your emergency fund, you could use a credit card as a short-term backup.

If you go down this path, though, it's important to understand that your credit card is for emergencies ONLY. It doesn't belong in your purse or wallet. It belongs in the back of your sock drawer at home, to be dusted off only in real emergencies. (And please note that not having enough money for a side of haloumi to go with your Sunday brunch is NOT an emergency.)

If you have all these areas covered, you can invest with confidence. You know you can 'ride out' any extended downturn in investment markets, simply waiting until your investments go back up in value before you sell. And you'll make more money over time, because you can let your investments grow over the right time period.

Cash also sucks

You should be aware that there's also a darker side to cash, and it's one most people blindly accept without thinking about. As an investment to grow your assets over time, cash is terrible.

The one exception to this is when you're older and about to retire (or in retirement), and you care about not losing money. Then, cash is great because it's very stable. But when you're trying to grow your money and build your assets, you should care more about growth than about stability.

As an investment to grow your assets over time, cash is terrible.

Cash gives you peace of mind. You can see it. You understand it. And if you're saving regularly, you can see it growing over time. But appearances can be deceiving: if you only invest in cash, your investments can actually end up going backwards because of tax and inflation.

I'm going to get a little technical here but bear with me ...

Remember that in Australia, you pay tax on all of your income — including your investment and interest on cash savings income — at your marginal tax rate. This tax rate depends on your income level, but if you earn more than $45 000 each year you're paying at least 32 per cent of every dollar you earn above that in tax.

The headline interest rate you receive from your bank is your 'pre-tax' interest rate. But the investment return you *actually* receive (and the one you should care most about) is the after-tax return. As the name suggests, this is the return you actually end up with after you've paid the tax on your investment income. So what does this mean in reality?

I've outlined an example with some formulas you can use to confirm your own after-tax return (on any investment) below:

After-tax return = pre-tax return − tax paid on the return

After-tax return = (100% − marginal tax rate) × pre-tax return

Pre-tax return (on Australian cash) = 3.1% (this is the 10-year average long-term return on cash in Australia in 2017)

Marginal tax rate = 32% (assuming annual income above $45 000)

After-tax return (on Australian cash) = 3.1% × 68% (100% − 32%)

After-tax return (on Australian cash) = 2.11%

You can see the after-tax return on a cash savings account is just over 2 per cent, which is around a third less than the headline return you see advertised. And the worst part is that this tax is often hidden.

With interest income from Australian bank accounts, you get the full (pre-tax) return paid into your account. Then, when you do your tax return at the end of the financial year, your interest income is added to your total taxable income, and the amount of tax you need to pay is calculated. The tax you pay on your interest reduces your after-tax return, or in some cases means you might actually have to pay extra tax. As a result, most people think they've got a bad accountant or that their employer is calculating their tax incorrectly. They don't realise the extra tax comes from the interest they've earned on their savings.

The other thing that impacts the 'real' return you receive on any investment (including cash) is inflation: the way general living expenses increase over time. I know we're getting a little jargon-y here, but understanding these terms is critical to understand the impact of the choices you're making with your money. The current inflation rate in Australia is 4.1 per cent, and the long-term average ranges between 2–3 per cent.

The rise in prices is important to consider when you invest because it impacts the purchasing power of your investments. For example, imagine you invest $10 000 today, and in ten years' time it's worth $500 000. Is this a good result? Well it definitely sounds like a good outcome, but what if I told you that ten years from now, a cup of coffee would cost you $100? Is your investment return still a good one?

You'd need to look at the numbers to know for sure, and the numbers you'd need to look at are the increase in prices vs the increase in your investment. This is what's called the 'real return'.

I mentioned above that your after-tax return is more important than your pre-tax return. But the most important return of all is your 'real' return: the after-tax return you get after accounting for inflation. Here's how you'd calculate this:

Real return = after-tax return − inflation

Real return = 2.11% − 4.1%

Real return = −1.99%

What happens when we look at the 'real' return on this savings investment example above? It's actually NEGATIVE. Not very negative, but negative all the same. This means if you'd kept all of your savings in cash over the last ten years in this example, you wouldn't have increased your investment pool at all. In fact it would have gone slightly backwards in 'real terms'.

This is like a death of a thousand cuts. Your savings balance increases, but you're not making any money in real terms. The worst part is that your psychology is working against you: you see your bank account balance going up, but don't see the tax being paid at the back end or inflation eating away at your hard-earned cash. So you feel good that your savings are growing, but you're really selling yourself short.

This is a serious risk for any money strategy. If you hold most of your savings in cash at the bank, you probably aren't making any gains AT ALL. In other words, saving cash is not a suitable long-term strategy to grow your assets over time. You need to do something smarter with your money.

Yes, cash is absolutely critical to every smart money strategy, and you'll need access to it to have confidence in your strategy and be able to sleep at night. But cash can also be an ineffective investment when you consider tax and inflation. Don't let the hidden nature of tax and inflation stop you from making real money.

Don't let the hidden nature of tax and inflation stop you from making real money.

The good news is that you're in the right place, and over the next few chapters we'll cover different types of investments that can help you actually make progress over time.

PUTTING IT ALL TOGETHER

Your tax position and cash savings are two of the foundational building blocks of your money strategy. They impact all the other money choices you make; and as with all money areas, you need to educate yourself to get the best results possible.

Tax can be really confusing and complex, so consider getting some good advice around this. Once you're across all the relevant information, you can take back control if you have the time and inclination. But until you get fully up-to-speed, you're probably leaving money on the table and paying more tax than you have to. That's why you should get on top of your tax strategy before making any big investment choices: it can be difficult and expensive to unwind things after you get started.

A good cash strategy will help you invest with confidence. It will give you peace of mind that the unexpected won't cause any huge financial problems. You need cash; but too much of anything is a bad thing—even sweet, sweet cash.

If you hold too much cash, you'll likely end up paying extra tax. AND, while your savings balance will increase over time, your actual 'real' (after inflation) asset values will probably go backwards. Take the time to optimise your cash strategy and you'll position yourself to get the most out of where you're at now.

CHAPTER 10

Don't shoot the lights out

Investing *can* be sexy. Companies like Facebook, Google, Apple and others have seen huge growth in the value of their companies and shares over time. We hear stories about high-flying stockbrokers and traders who make enormous sums of money in a very short amount of time by trading shares. They pick the right companies at the right time, invest money in them, and then sell those investments at a huge gain.

It sounds amazing. It sounds fun. It sounds sexy. It sounds like an easy way to make a lot of money fast. No doubt this is why so many people try to trade and make their own millions through this sort of investing.

But it doesn't always work this way. In 2008, a trader (professional investor) and employee of Societe Generale, one of Europe's largest banks, lost over US$7 billion (yes, with a 'b') through bad investment decisions. This trader was a professional investor who'd been working in the bank for years, so he couldn't blame a lack of experience for the losses.

A court later found that he'd acted fraudulently to cover up his trading and the resulting losses. Societe Generale apparently wasn't aware of the position he'd taken, or the bets he'd made on the markets. But how did he get it so wrong? Even for one of Europe's largest banks, $7 billion is a huge sum of money to lose through bad investment decisions.

Over a period of around two years, this trader had made a series of these bad decisions. And instead of 'fessing up' to his losses, he tried to cover his tracks. He made even more investments (read: bets) in an attempt to make back the money he'd lost. He failed.

So how did a single individual almost wipe out one of Europe's oldest and largest banks? The allure of investment markets and the thrill of picking a winner had landed this trader in jail, lost him his marriage (and his job and career). The interesting thing was that the trader didn't even stand to personally benefit from the investments he'd made. Even if he'd been right, and those investments had made a stack of money, he wouldn't have personally benefitted.

It just goes to show how strong the pull of investment markets can be.

On a smaller scale, I met a client a few years ago—I'll call him Beau. Beau had taken an interest in investing, started reading books and doing online courses on the topic, and followed investment markets closely. And after undertaking quite a lot of research over a two-year period, he'd started investing himself. He started small, taking small risks, and making small profits (and sometimes small losses).

On balance, he was making more than he was losing, and was learning about investment markets—so he felt he was onto something. He'd started out investing in ordinary shares, but then moved on to more complex investments like options, currency, and ultimately precious metals (gold, silver, platinum, etc.)

He really enjoyed this investing, and his investment portfolio was building up nicely. Before too long, he'd started investing more, looking to ramp up how much money he was making. He hoped that if he could learn enough and make enough money through investing, he'd be able to quit his nine-to-five job. The dream of day trading in his underwear between strolls to the local cafe and mani-pedis was in sight.

It *sounded* like a good plan at the time.

But what Beau—like so many others before him—found is that being successful with this sort of investing long-term is hard. Investment markets do have rules, trends, and historical behaviours and performance that give us some insight into what might happen in the future.

But that insight doesn't mean you can always get it right. The people who participate in investment markets (and ultimately drive the behaviour and returns of those markets) are just people. And people sometimes do strange things. They're hard to predict.

I met a guy once who used to eat the skin on avocados. My uncle has an entire suit made from linen. Another guy I know doesn't like looking at plants with pointy leaves because they make him dizzy. Like I said, people are weird. They do irrational, crazy things—seriously, who eats the skin on avocados???

Essentially, when you invest, you're aiming to 'beat' other investors. For you to make money, someone else has to lose. So unless you can accurately predict what everyone else is going to do, it's difficult to consistently 'win' at investing.

It didn't end so well for Beau. He made a couple of not-so-great decisions and got a little unlucky with his timing. He first lost all the profits he'd made from his investments, and then shortly afterwards lost the amount he'd started with (which was his retirement savings).

Fortunately, he was only 40 when he lost those savings. With some hard work and commitment, he had enough time to correct his course and recover financially. He was annoyed at himself for those losses, but we got him back on track so that he (and his wife) were once again happy. Of course, without that setback, he could have either reached the same position sooner and more easily, or reached an even better position.

Stories of people like the Societe Generale trader are rare, while those like Beau's are much more common. It's easy to get caught up in the allure of investing. You imagine cracking the code of the markets so you can make money in your pyjamas in just a few hours each day. You think about all the free time you'll have to play golf, brunch with your mates, or maybe hit up the day spa.

While the scale was different, both Beau and our mate at Societe Generale were following a similar investment strategy. They were trying to 'beat' the market, thinking they knew better than all the other investors out there. Their strategy wasn't to make longer-term money by buying good investments and holding them over time as they increased in value. Instead, they were looking to make big money fast through short-term investing.

This sort of investing involves more risk than your standard 'buy and hold' strategy. Why? Because you're trying to make money using some technique, information or strategy that other investors don't know about.

Carl Richards sums this up in his book *The Behaviour Gap*: 'Trying to pick the performance of a share or company based on past performance is like trying to pick whether a coin toss will come up heads or tails when you know the last result. The previous toss tells you nothing.'

It's easy to get caught up in the hype surrounding the stories of others who've invested and done it all before (and so easily of course). But what are the chances of getting it right? And—perhaps more importantly—what are the consequences of getting it wrong?

Remember: people dedicate their entire working lives to trying to crack the investing code, and still don't get it right. For the average person with a few spare hours each week, their only hope is to get super lucky.

Survivorship bias

Just the other day, I saw a social media advert from a trader who talked about how he'd made a lot of money. Now he was selling an online training course to teach his 'foolproof' method for getting the same results. And he's far from the only one.

So I hear you asking, if these people can do it, why can't I?

'Survivorship bias' is a term that describes the effect where people who've failed at something fade away, leaving only the ones who've succeeded. For example, if you looked at the growth of all existing companies now that were startups ten years ago, this group wouldn't include the *many* failed businesses that had gone bust in the ten-year period. The growth of those remaining companies would then look much better than if you'd included the full group of ALL the startups.

Each year, there are hundreds of thousands, if not millions of new investors around the world. And these investors all have dreams of making it big, retiring early, and probably buying a yacht and living the high life.

How does survivorship bias affect the stories of these investors? Imagine that 100 000 people each bet $1000 on a coin toss. Half bet on heads, and half on tails. When the coin is tossed, half of those people will be correct. So that leaves 50 000 'successful' investors in the coin toss who've now doubled their money to $2000.

Then the coin is tossed again, and again half of the 'investors' bet each way. So, after the toss, again half will be correct, leaving 25 000 'successful' investors each with $4000. A third round has the same results, leaving 12 500 'success' stories of people who've each made $8000 from their initial $1000.

By now, you're probably getting the hang of this. After 15 rounds of betting, only three investors would have guessed correctly each time. In the process, they would have built their $1000 up to a whopping $32 768 000. But of course, the other side of the story is that the remaining 99 997 investors would have all lost their $1000 and now have nothing.

If you heard of someone who'd made over $32m after starting with just $1000, would you buy their eBook? The people who get this right seem like geniuses. That or they have some sort of special powers that allow them to correctly predict the toss of a coin 15 times in a row. Everyone looks to them in awe. We think they must be able to predict the future, read minds, or at least tell us how to get our office crush to pay more attention to us. We try to figure out how they did it … and think about what *we'd* do with $32m we earned from $1000.

> **We all have an inbuilt tendency to remember the success stories much more easily.**

We all have an inbuilt tendency to remember the success stories much more easily. This is because we get caught up imagining how the successful person could be us. We hold onto that thought. We'd rather not think about losing all our money, so we selectively forget the stories of failure and instead focus on the ones that lead to success.

The coin toss example shows survivorship bias in action. The players in this game had no real skills. Their results were due purely to chance probability. If enough people try to predict the outcome of an event, some of them will always be correct. And if enough of them make different predictions on a string of events, a small group of people will eventually predict correctly each time.

This doesn't represent prediction skill. It's simply the law of large numbers.

And this basic example holds true for all investing. It's even easier to look like an investment genius in real life because you DON'T usually 'bet' all your money on each investment. Instead, you only use a portion, so getting your investment choice wrong doesn't mean going completely bust. That means you have more opportunities to make back any money lost, return to genius status, and in turn look like a huge success story.

Don't be fooled by our survivorship bias tendency to more easily recall success stories. Nobody can predict the future accurately all of the time. For every success story, there are a hundred others about people who either performed poorly and lost it all or gave up.

So many people start investing in these sorts of exotic investments, thinking that it will be 'fun' and that they'll make big money fast. If you want a fun hobby, my suggestion is to join a gym, take up online gaming, or join the local taco appreciation society. Don't choose one that could put your savings and future at risk.

(I sincerely apologise if I've crushed your dreams of being a high-flying day trader in your underwear.)

How much risk do you need?

So you're probably never going to become one of these 'get rich quick' stories. You'll never make $1m in a day's trading. And you won't be able to start that side hustle selling your trading secrets on Facebook once you've cracked the code.

I know that wasn't what you wanted to hear. It's not sexy. It's not exciting. But it's still true. Ask yourself, though: do you really *need* to get rich quick?

Investing *will* make you money. Quite a lot of it if you're smart. But that money won't come fast. It won't come easy. And it won't come at all unless you have a solid strategy, follow through, and have some patience.

Investing isn't supposed to be 'sexy'. It's not supposed to be 'fun'. It can definitely be enjoyable, and making money is always rewarding, but investing isn't a game. When you invest smart, think about how much risk you actually NEED to take to get the investment outcomes you want.

Your investment strategy should be smart, considered, growth-focused, and boring.

Aim to run an investment strategy that's as boring as possible. The more boring your investments are, the less risk you're likely to face. I'm not saying you shouldn't have growth-focused investments, or that you shouldn't expect to make good money. They just don't need to be EXCITING. There's hobbies for that. Instead, your investment strategy should be smart, considered, growth-focused, and boring.

When you invest, you should have already thought about what success looks like. But most people invest without any actual investment goals. They don't think about what their measure of success is. They just want to make money. Lots of money. As much as possible. And as quickly as possible.

If you're not clear on what success looks like, you'll never know whether your investments are doing 'well', 'poorly', or 'just okay'. This seems a little crazy to me now, although I must admit that when I was in university making my first investments, I didn't have any investment goals either. I just wanted to make a bunch of money. I secretly hoped my investments would skyrocket, making me enough money to quit my job and 'study' at uni full time without the heavy weight of working two four-hour shifts a week at the pub. But I never clarified what that might look like. If I did, I would have realised my goals were insane, and that so was the risk I was facing.

Without a measure of success, you end up looking at the performance of your investments vs the performance of the best-performing investments. This is a cruel game that leads to constant feelings of inadequacy. You might be doing well, but there are always other people doing better.

There's also a bigger problem in play here. When you invest, there's a direct relationship between the amount of money you can reasonably expect to make (your investment return), and the level of risk involved. If you want to make 'loads' from every investment, you'll face higher and higher levels of risk. You'll end up being drawn to investments you think will make you big bucks, but which run a higher risk of striking out and losing you your money.

If, on the other hand, you look forward and assess the investment outcomes you want or need, you might be surprised. Let me illustrate.

The long-term return on Australian shares for the last 20 years was 8.7 per cent. The table below shows the return you'd get if you were to invest $10 into the Australian share market every day, and then reinvest the profits and income generated over this time.

$10/day investment	10 years Total $36 500 invested	20 years Total $73 000 invested	30 years Total $109 500 invested	40 years Total $146 000 invested
Australian Shares	$54 666	$180 564	$470 506	$1 138 245

So over 20 years, you can reasonably expect to double your money. Over 30 years, it would more than quadruple. And if you had a 40-year timeline you'd expect your invested amount to increase more than seven times over. Not bad, right? And again, $10 each day isn't a huge investment for most young professionals. But what if you invested a little more?

The table below shows the impact if you could find more than that, and how each level of money could grow over time. Of course, the past doesn't necessarily predict the future, but these numbers do give us a fair indication of the sorts of outcomes you could reasonably expect.

	10 years	20 years	30 years	40 years
$20/day investment	$109 332	$361 128	$941 012	$2 276 490
$50/day investment	$273 330	$902 820	$2 352 530	$5 691 225
$100/day investment	$546 660	$1 805 640	$4 705 060	$11 382 450

The relationship between investment amount and returns is linear. If you double your investment, your returns will double. For most people, this sort of return is enough to deliver the money results they want. In fact, most people could get where they want to be by getting returns lower than the market average. You don't *need* to try to pick the next Apple, Google or Facebook to get rich.

It's like when you meet a cute guy or girl at a bar. You think they might have some interest. You catch a couple of glimpses from them across the room. You're feeling good. They're looking good. You want their phone number. So if you're going to take action to make it happen, you have two main options at this point.

First, you could think of something semi-clever to say to them and start a conversation. You could play it cool, try to start a conversation, and hope your awesome strategy comes through and they give up their phone number. The risk for this option is pretty low.

The second option has much higher stakes. You could go ask the DJ to put on your favourite Kanye track, clear a space on the dancefloor, start getting your full groove on, and put on a show. You could work it so hard that you look like a dance god or goddess. And if you get the dance right, your sweetheart will fall apart with desire and ask you to marry them on the spot.

That's IF you pull off the dance.

A far more probable outcome, of course, is that you stuff up your dance. Your timing is wrong. Someone gets in your way and you have to adjust your dance routine on the go. Or you're just a crap dancer. And when this happens, you look like a total fool and ruin any chance you had with your crush.

So how much risk do you need? The first option is fairly safe and conservative. It has a higher chance of getting you the outcome you want. The second option is fraught with danger and has the potential for an even higher reward...but the likely outcome is total failure and misery.

Pro Tip

The figures above show that you don't need to take on huge amounts of risk to make good money over time with investing. So don't risk losing your hard-earned savings by effectively 'betting' on which investments will shoot the lights out next. A good investment strategy involves figuring out how much money you need, and then plotting a course to get there with the LOWEST possible level of risk. Don't take on more risk than you need to get the results you want.

When you're setting up your investment strategy, what you 'want' is less important than what you 'need'. We're all human, so of course you want to invest in the best company, get the biggest returns, and have that great story to tell your mates at your next catch up. But ask yourself how much you really need.

When you're setting up your investment strategy, what you 'want' is less important than what you 'need'.

I'd suggest that one thing you 'need' to do is make sure you don't risk losing a big chunk (or all) of your cash by trying to pick investments that will shoot the lights out.

Once you understand that you don't need to take huge risks to get the money results that are important to you, you need to know a few things for smart investing. I've covered these below, and I'll get a little complex and technical here, but bear with me.

These are important, and understanding them will be a big step towards investing like a pro and getting the right investment results for you. That said, if you don't completely understand them, don't stress. Any financial adviser you work with should be across this information. And a limited understanding will help you know what questions to ask them to get you the best investment results.

Investment timing: volatility

As I mentioned in Chapter 9, shares (or the managed investment funds that invest in shares) go up and down in value. This often happens many times each day. The amount that they go up and down by is called 'volatility', so an investment with a lot of ups and downs is said to have high volatility. On the flip side, a more stable investment with fewer ups and downs is said to have low volatility.

This volatility is the natural order of things. You can't expect investments to stay at the same value from one day to another. In fact, if they do, there's probably something wrong. The 'trick' with investing is to understand these ups and downs and their impact on investments.

When you understand that investments go up and down at different times, you know that you never want to be forced to sell your investments when they're 'down'. This means you need to understand your investment timeline risk. For example, when you buy any share-type investment, it's possible that the markets will crash the very next day, and the value of your investments will crash with it (see diagram below).

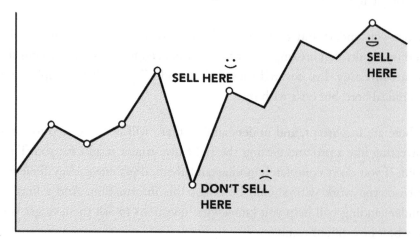

You'd have to be a little unlucky for this to happen, but it's possible. And if this scenario did happen, you'd need the ability to 'wait out' the market until it recovered so you could get the return you wanted on your investments. This means you *need* to get your investment timeline right.

If you don't have a long enough investment timeframe to wait for the investments to go back up in value (i.e. you need the money for something else), you'll become a 'forced seller' and lose money on your investment. Think Eve and Riley with their house in Chapter 6. But if you have enough time—and of course, a good investment to start with—all you have to do is wait for the market to recover and you'll be back ahead.

When you invest money, think through how long you can leave it invested for. For shares and managed funds, the suggested time frame is ten years or more. This is because when share markets have tanked around the world in the past, they've usually recovered within that time.

And that's why your investment strategy needs to link back to your saving and spending strategy, which depends on you having a solid saving and spending strategy BEFORE you invest. That strategy will give you confidence that you've provided for all the spending that's important to you, so you can confidently invest knowing you've got money to cover all the spending you want to do.

That being said, of course you don't HAVE to keep your investments for ten years. If your investments are increasing in value, you can sell them at any time and be 'in front'. If your money is invested for long-term wealth-building, you shouldn't need to sell your investments. But if their value is up and you wanted to sell them for some reason (like making a different investment), you absolutely could—and you'd come out ahead. It's only if your investments are going down in value that you need to be able to hold them until markets recover so you don't lose money.

Diversification

Diversification involves spreading your risk across different investments to reduce the effects of volatility, and smooth your investment returns over time. It's one of the most effective risk management strategies you can use in your investment strategy.

When you invest in one company, the return you get is simply the return for that particular company. But when you invest in two companies, the return you get becomes the average of the returns on each of the companies. This is shown in the diagram below:

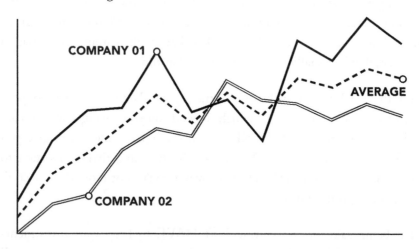

In other words, investing in more companies makes the line showing your returns smoother. There are fewer ups and downs overall because the ups and downs of any one investment are balanced by the ups and downs of all the other investments in your portfolio.

The more individual investments you include in your portfolio, the smoother your investment returns will be. Importantly, the more individual investments you have in your portfolio, the less impact any one company's performance will have on your overall return.

If one company performs really well, you'll benefit — just not as much as if you'd only invested in that one company. But on the flip side, if one company or investment performs really poorly (or goes bust), that will also have less of an impact on your overall return. This is a powerful risk management strategy. If you diversify enough, you can effectively eliminate individual company risk, and be left with just 'market risk'.

The more individual investments you include in your portfolio, the smoother your investment returns will be.

When I advise clients, I always recommend a highly diversified investment approach because they'll end up with smoother returns and lower levels of risk. It does mean they won't have that one investment that shoots the lights out and makes them rich overnight, but it also helps them sleep better knowing their investment risk is lower.

What is a managed fund?

A managed fund is an investment fund run on behalf of investors by an agent or investment management company. Think of it as a group of investors coming together to invest money, with a professional investment manager helping to choose investments and then doing all the administration. Because these funds are normally quite large (at least $5m, with most over $100m), you get benefits from pooling your money together with multiple other investors.

Each investor owns a small portion of the overall managed fund. The money they use to 'buy in' to the fund is used to purchase investments in line with its investment strategy. There are over 10 000 different managed funds in Australia, all investing in different ways and following different investment strategies. Some track the overall market, while others might focus on investing only in technology companies. And still others might invest in commodities like coffee, wheat or other agricultural produce.

One of the big benefits of a managed fund is that you can get started with less money and still follow a highly diversified investment strategy. If you want to invest $500 directly in shares, the costs involved mean it often only makes sense to buy a single share or a small number of them. When you invest the same amount into a managed fund, you still have one investment (the managed fund), but that in turn invests in hundreds or thousands of other shares.

Another benefit of managed funds is scale, because more money and more people involved mean you can spread the cost of doing the investment management and research over more people. These funds also get good deals when they buy and sell shares, so costs are lower than if you did it all yourself.

Managed funds can be a low-cost, diversified investment option that lets you get started straight away. There are heaps of options, so set your investment strategy before you jump in (I cover this below). But once your strategy is sorted, look at which managed funds are available, and see whether one could work for you.

Pro Tip

Your investment solutions should ALWAYS follow from your structure and strategy, so get these two areas sorted BEFORE you make any investment (including managed funds).

Active vs passive investing

When you invest, you need to decide on the sort of investment strategy you want to follow. When it comes to choosing this, you'll come across two main styles: active and passive. It's important to understand these options so you can make the choice that's right for you.

Active investing

As the name suggests, active investing means your investments are managed 'actively'. When you actively invest, you choose investments that you think will do better and perform more strongly than all the other investments out there.

This normally involves working with a fund manager who runs analyses to figure out which companies will and won't perform well. You then choose more of these companies, and (try to) avoid any that will experience average performance or go backwards. In short, an active investor assumes they can do better than all the other investors by choosing the best companies to invest money in.

If you want to be an active investor, you can invest directly into shares and set up a portfolio with the share investments you think will perform best. Another option is to use a managed fund with an investment management company that specialises in active investment management.

Passive investing

The alternative approach is passive investing, which as the name suggests involves passively investing in the share market. In contrast to active investing, you simply invest into a managed fund that follows the overall market (i.e. all companies).

Once you do this, you're (almost*) certain to get the average return of the market you're investing in. All the information on all the companies in every share market worldwide is publicly available, so it's easy enough for a managed fund to replicate the return of any given share market. These funds use complex algorithms to pull the publicly available information and automatically invest so the managed investment fund duplicates the market it's tracking.

Note: The only slight deviation from perfect replication of the market is what's called a 'tracking error'. This error is created because index funds can't track the market in perfect time: they need the information to be reported before they adjust the investments in the fund. The tracking error is very small (around 0.2 per cent on average) so this isn't something you need to worry about. However, it's technically incorrect to say an index investment perfectly replicates the market, so I wanted to include this here.

Indices

The image below shows a pie chart of the 200 largest companies in Australia based on their value. The information on these companies, including their names and value, is all publicly available at www.marketindex.com .au/asx200.

If you had $2.62 trillion (give or take), you could use that money to buy up all of these 200 companies. If you did this, the return you'd get on your investment would be the combined return of these 200 companies, which as we've talked about in previous examples is 8.7 per cent p.a. over the last 20 years for the Australian share market.

Of course, most people don't have $2.62 trillion to invest. But if you want to get the same return on a smaller amount of money, there is a solution. As we discussed above, all the information on global markets is publicly available so you can use it to invest a smaller amount of money and get the same results. As long as you get the percentages correct, your results will be the same. At least in theory anyway: in practice, you'd still need a pretty large amount of money to get all the percentages correct and invest in all 200 companies.

And *that's* where index funds come in.

An 'index' is a measure of the value (and changes in the value) of share investments that represent some or all of the overall market. One index, which represents the 200 largest companies in Australia, is called the ASX200.

This is what you see each night when the finance newsreader says the Australian share market or ASX has gone up by 1 per cent.

In the diagram below, you can see the value of the ASX200 at the time of writing, as well as the biggest companies, their current values, and the implied percentage of the total value of the overall market they represent.

All an index fund does is gather up this publicly available information and set up an algorithm to invest the money in the index fund consistent with the same percentages of the overall market. These algorithms allow index funds to replicate the market or index they are tracking almost perfectly.

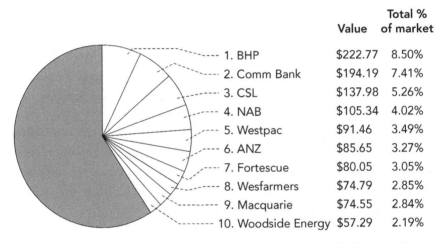

	Value	Total % of market
1. BHP	$222.77	8.50%
2. Comm Bank	$194.19	7.41%
3. CSL	$137.98	5.26%
4. NAB	$105.34	4.02%
5. Westpac	$91.46	3.49%
6. ANZ	$85.65	3.27%
7. Fortescue	$80.05	3.05%
8. Wesfarmers	$74.79	2.85%
9. Macquarie	$74.55	2.84%
10. Woodside Energy	$57.29	2.19%

Total value: AUD$2.62 trillion

If you want to follow a passive investment approach and create your own share portfolio, you'll find it very difficult to track the market correctly yourself without a big pile of cash to invest. Plus, this strategy requires either a really smart algorithm, or a lot of work, monitoring and regular adjustment to ensure your portfolio consistently follows the market.

A much better option is to use a managed fund that specialises in passive investment. There are many of these: the largest is Blackrock, and the second largest is Vanguard. Both are based in the US. However, you can invest in passive index funds for almost any share market around the world.

There are many Australian index funds, US index funds, and funds for individual countries in Europe, Asia, and the rest of the world. You can also invest in region-based index funds, i.e. North or South America, Europe, Asia, etc. There are even some that cover the whole world.

Pros and cons of active vs passive investing (hint: both have risks)

Active investing

The main 'benefit' or promise of active funds is that they aim to deliver returns above those of the market overall. The biggest risk with active investing is that the investments you choose might not perform as expected. Because these investments are chosen by humans and there's no secret formula to predict the future and choose the best companies, this is a very real risk.

I read an article recently that analysed the results of one of the 'top' online investment research companies, which publishes an annual report on their best investment picks. This article found that if you'd invested in their best picks, your return would have been significantly lower than the market return (more than 3 per cent lower over a year).

These findings are supported by research from Vanguard, an investment giant and research company, who also recently analysed the performance of professional investment managers over the longer-term. They found that over 70 per cent of investment managers fail to do better than the market return over a five year period (see bibliography for link to Vanguard Research).

If the professional investors — global giant investment powerhouses with virtually unlimited resources and a huge amount of experience — can't get it right, what hope does an ordinary person or investment adviser have? This shows that you need to be *really* careful when looking for tips to invest.

Be aware that if you follow an active investment strategy, you run the real risk of the person making your investment decisions getting them wrong, and you suffering the consequences through lower returns and potentially losses.

Active investments also generally cost more. Active investment managers usually either employ large teams of investment analysts, or spend loads on technology to crunch their numbers and figure out which investments will perform best. They also probably have an investment committee or board made up of heavy hitters from the industry.

I don't know if you've ever met an active fund manager, but I have. They wear really nice suits. They drive really nice cars. They have really nice houses. And good luck to them. But at the end of the day, it's their investors who pay for their Ferraris and mansions.

Active investments can be much more stressful too. When you use an active investment approach, you have to hope the person making the investment decisions is getting this right. Because an active investment manager never really KNOWS whether their investment decision will work out the way they think it will, you'll be sweating on the result. If your active investment manager gets it wrong, you lose money.

Finally, active investments require a LOT of time. Whether you use an active investment manager or manage your investment portfolio yourself, you need to constantly review your investments, and decide whether you should hold, sell, or buy more. This can be extremely time-consuming (not to mention difficult).

For some people, though, all those downsides feel as though they're worth the potential payoff.

One benefit of active investments that's worth noting is that some of these funds hold different types of investments that can be used to reduce risk. This can be particularly useful for people who are about to retire or are in retirement, who are extremely concerned with risk management. In this instance, active investment funds should be seriously considered as a risk management strategy.

Passive investing

Meanwhile, the downside of a passive investment strategy is that investing in the entire market won't get you the huge returns that are possible when you put all your money into fewer investments.

But on the flip side, you also reduce the risk of investment failure. Because you're investing in the overall market, the only way your investment can fail (go to $0) is if the entire market fails (read: nuclear winter or the apocalypse). The chances of this happening are very low, and if it did happen you'd have bigger issues than failed investments.

This means you don't have to stress about your investments, and can be confident in the knowledge your money is invested in the market itself so you're not making 'bets'. You KNOW what your investment will do: it will only ever track the market the fund is investing in. That means you can sleep soundly at night, knowing you're going to get the returns of the market. Every. Single. Day.

If a client ever asks me how their investments are doing, my answer is always the same: 'Your investments are doing what the markets are doing.' This additional peace of mind means you can get on with the other things that are important to you, and save your concern for other things in your life.

Passive index funds are also highly diversified. Because you're investing in the total market, you end up with hundreds and sometimes even thousands of individual investments. This level of diversification reduces the impact of any one investment on the return of your overall portfolio.

Another benefit of using passive index investments is that they're very cheap. Their costs are limited to just their hardware and key staff. So passive investment managers really only need a team of cracking coders and a huge warehouse full of super computers (okay, and massive air conditioners to keep them cool).

This allows them to keep costs low and run a much more streamlined operation. The cost savings of passive funds go straight to your bottom line: the average cost of an index fund is less than 0.30 per cent p.a. So if you have $100k to invest, you'll pay less than $300 each year in fees.

Now, as I've mentioned a few times through this book, cost isn't everything. Most of the time you do need to pay for quality. But in the case of investment managers, there's hard evidence that shows they fail to perform as well as the market (or the passive index funds that replicate the market) most of the time. So this extra cost isn't justified in my opinion.

Finally, a passive investment approach will also save you a bunch of time when it comes to reviewing and managing your financial strategy. You do still need to review regularly if your situation or priorities change. But otherwise, once your passive investment strategy is set, your investment choices become pretty clear. You know passive index fund investments will *always* deliver what they say they will, so you don't need to spend loads of time, effort or money constantly reviewing your investment portfolio.

Basically, passive investments let you automate your investment strategy and save you time in the process.

Which strategy is right for you?

To figure out which is right for you, go back to the work you've done on how much risk you NEED to run in your strategy. That will help you to establish what sort of investment strategy is best for you.

But as I said earlier, when I'm advising clients, I always recommend a passive approach for the benefits outlined above. It reduces almost all investment risk other than the risk of the market and your timeline risk.

If you take the time to set up a solid strategy around your overall situation and investment plan, you'll manage your timeline risk well. This leaves you with only the market risk, which is what you WANT because it's what drives the returns you get from your money over time. This is why, when we're advising clients, we use almost exclusively passive investments.

Pro Tip

If you're in or very close to retirement, you might need to do things a little differently. In this case, actively managed funds can help to manage risk, which is super important when you don't have the time to recover if markets crash. Retirement planning is well outside the scope of this book—but if this is you, consider exploring further.

Basically, think through what you want to achieve with your investment strategy and which investment style suits you best. Get this decision right and you'll get the investment outcomes you want, save time and lower your stress levels because you'll know your investment strategy is solid.

PUTTING IT ALL TOGETHER

Investing will help you to replace your income over time, so if you don't want to work forever, you need a good strategy to grow your investments.

Our tendency toward greed is the second of the two powerful drivers of investment choices. As we covered above, it's common to want to get the most out of every investment you make. But if you push to shoot the lights out with your investments, you run the risk of losing it all. And if you can get solid returns over time that will get you to the results you want, why take on more risk?

So when you invest, set your strategy first. Benchmark what success in your investments looks like over time. See how those results fit with your wants, targets and goals. You'll probably be surprised how quickly you can get ahead if you stick to your strategy and simply get stable, steady returns over time. Greed is natural, but it will lead to momentum-killing setbacks and mistakes—if you let it.

Get solid around your planning so you don't let your psychology and decision-making biases get in the way of making smart investment choices.

CHAPTER 11

The house always wins (or does it?)

Early in your money journey when you're young, buying property is often seen as the first big step to adulting with money. Your parents have done it. Some of your mates, colleagues or family have done it too. And with the growth in Australian house prices over the last 50 years, everybody knows a bunch of success stories from people who've made loads of money investing in property.

But buying property is a big step that will have a long-term impact on your financial situation over time, so how do you get this big decision right?

There are things you need to understand about property to get clear on whether it's the right step for you to take. Then, if you're going to actually *buy*, there are more steps you need to take to get the outcomes you want. This chapter is all about helping you get clear on those critical factors, so when you choose to buy property you know you're going to be well placed for success.

What makes property good

I've spoken to loads of young people who want to buy property. In fact, almost every person I talk to about money has earmarked property as the next big step on their money journey.

But they often don't know why.

I'm not saying property *isn't* a good investment. It's just not the only investment. So I always ask people why they want to buy property, and why that reason is important to them. Most people tell me it's because they want to do something smart with their money. And property is usually the only investment they really understand.

I totally get this. If you don't understand how other investments work, it's natural to see them as more risky and be afraid of making a mistake. So often by process of elimination, property ends up being the best choice. And sometimes it is, but other times it's not.

Because of this, people view property as some magical investment that always generates strong returns. But this is not always the case.

The long-term return on Australian property from the ASX long-term investment report puts the total return on Australian residential property at 10.5 per cent. Remember that the return on Australian shares was 8.7 per cent. Both these figures are for the total return, including the increase in asset value, and the income return (rent or dividends) received.

In the table below, I've shown the return you'd receive through investing $500000 in Australian residential property vs in shares.

Shares vs property

	5 years	10 years	15 years
Shares – $500k invested @ 8.7%	$771270	$1189716	$1835184
Property – $500k invested @ 10.5%	$843301	$1422315	$2398880

You can see from these numbers that the difference in return is small at first, but it increases over time (the power of time and money is a wonderful thing…) So if you had $500k in the bank that you were looking to invest, in the early years it would be a close call as to which would make you more money.

Over the long-term, though, property becomes a clear winner. That said, the figures show that both options can make you a solid amount of money over time. The massive benefit of buying property is that pretty much everyone borrows money from the bank to do so. They put in some cash savings, borrow the rest, and get themselves a property.

(Yes, I've worked with a few people who've bought properties outright with cash. But most of them were retired—or almost retired—and had already built up their assets. It's extremely rare for someone to buy their first property using only cash they've saved.)

So why is borrowing to buy property a good thing? When you buy property, you're investing a small amount (your deposit) to buy a much larger asset (the property). As long as you choose the right property, its value should increase over time, while your mortgage will stay the same or—ideally—reduce. This accelerates how quickly your asset (the property) grows over time.

That's why, as we discussed in Chapter 9, it's often called 'gearing'. And it's this gearing that's the biggest benefit you get when investing in property.

But most people don't get clear on this before they invest. They see property as an awesome investment that will magically—and inevitably—make them money. It's not. It's simply the power of gearing that drives your returns on your property investment.

What makes property bad

Despite its gearing benefits, property isn't for everyone. And because it's such a big commitment, it's also an asset that can cause you a lot of pain. I've unfortunately met many people who've got their property strategy wrong and suffered as a result. Remember Riley & Eve in Chapter 6? These people's stories often featured the same factors, so it's important to understand those factors BEFORE you jump into buying property.

Entry and exit costs are high

Typical costs to buy a property run at around 5 per cent of its value. This includes stamp duty (the biggest cost), legal fees, property title searches and other random purchase costs. The exact costs will depend on where you buy your property and what government incentives are available through 'first home buyer' and other grants. But 5 per cent is a good conservative estimate.

Selling a property is also expensive. You need to pay for the real estate agent (the biggest cost) as well as legals, title transfers and other costs. Again, a conservative estimate of these costs would be 5 per cent of the property's value.

So if you buy a property and then need to sell it, you'll lose around 10 per cent of its value straight up. That means if you buy and sell a $500k property, the total costs would be around $50k. Losing this sort of money early on in your money journey is a serious momentum-killer.

Mortgage payments will put a dent in your spending

When you buy your first property, you'll probably have a pretty big mortgage — so ongoing payments are likely to be equally hefty. Mortgage interest rates often increase over time (depending on the property cycle), which can put further pressure on your budget. On top of your mortgage, you need to factor in ongoing property costs like strata fees, council and land rates, and property maintenance.

All this means that when you transition from paying rent to funding the entire cost of the mortgage yourself, the cost of your housing can increase hugely.

You need to choose the right asset

This last one is perhaps one of the most painful. If you don't choose the right property, you can suffer through years of slow or no growth. This puts you into the very difficult position of wanting to sell the property, but not wanting to lose money. So you get emotionally attached to the investment, and frustration ensues.

We're going to dive deep into how to choose the right property investment in this chapter. That way, you'll know exactly what to look for and what questions to ask yourself to choose a great property when you buy.

So what can you do?

When you buy property, you need a solid strategy to avoid being forced to sell at a time that's not ideal.

You need to think through the budget impact of your purchase to make sure it comfortably fits and won't put you into a position you don't want to be in. You also need to factor in a buffer for mortgage rates increasing, so any future rate rises don't put additional pressure on your budget.

And, as we discussed above, you need to choose the right property: one that will be solid and make you money over time.

If you look at the numbers and find you'll be stretched to buy a property, remember that our shares vs property example above shows shares are a good investment that can deliver strong returns over time too. You don't need to push yourself to buy property *now*.

Instead, you can get started with the sorts of share-type investments we discussed in Chapter 10, build your assets, and then buy property in the future when you're in a more comfortable position. You'll still make money and you'll still end up with a property, but you'll do it without the extra pressure and stress that comes with being stretched to the limit.

Pro Tip

Don't stretch yourself to buy property you can't afford AS WELL AS the other spending you want to do. Rushing in when you're not ready can cause years of pain and slow progress.

How to buy property like a pro

Once you're confident that property *is* the right step for you to take, there are also some key things you need to know to get your investment right. When you buy, you should follow a process to get the results you want from your purchase. It's absolutely, 100 per cent critical to follow these steps in order.

How to Buy Property Like a Pro

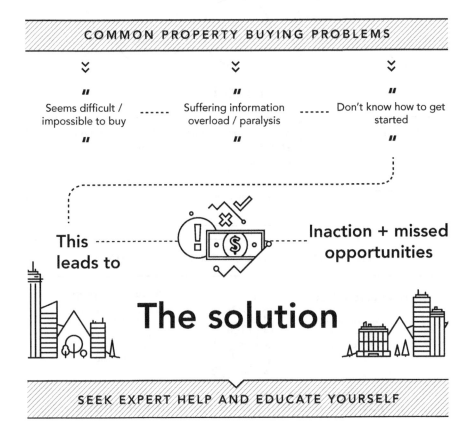

" Seems difficult / impossible to buy "

" Suffering information overload / paralysis "

" Don't know how to get started "

This leads to

Inaction + missed opportunities

The solution

FOUR KEY QUESTIONS YOU SHOULD ANSWER:

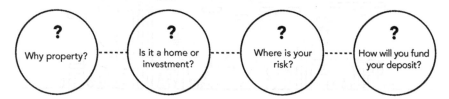

? Why property? - - - - **?** Is it a home or investment? - - - - **?** Where is your risk? - - - - **?** How will you fund your deposit?

Once you've answered these questions you can set up your perfect property strategy to give you the money and lifestyle outcomes you want

THIS WILL HELP YOU CLARIFY

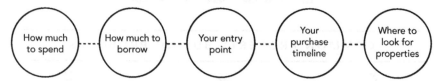

How much to spend - - - How much to borrow - - - Your entry point - - - Your purchase timeline - - - Where to look for properties

Then

Build your team.	Set your borrowing strategy.	Research your market.
- Financial Adviser - Broker - Lawyer - Buyer's agent?	(your broker/laywer/adviser will work with you to decide) - Fixed vs Variable - Offset vs redraw - Interest only vs P+I	- Areas - Types of properties - Features

FIND YOUR PERFECT PROPERTY THEN

Negotiate + Secure

- Due diligence
- Bid + Offer
- Pay deposit

Pre purchase prep

(your laywer/adviser will work with you to get your)

- Loan approved
- Contracts
- Settlement

Enjoy the benefits of a great investment!

Some clients I worked with a while back—let's call them Anthony and Mia—got this wrong. Anthony and Mia were a young couple in their early 30s who'd just had their first child. They wanted to buy a property and had been looking around, but weren't confident about their strategy, so needed some help.

They told me what was important to them and the sorts of properties they'd been looking at. I started analysing the numbers, and met with Anthony and Mia to talk the analysis through with them. But when we caught up, they nervously told me they'd been to an auction on the weekend, had found the perfect place, and had put a bid on the property.

Their bid had been accepted. That was when I discovered the problem.

They'd looked at properties previously, and had found a few they liked but nothing that ticked all the boxes. And then they did … except that the price point was a little higher than they'd originally looked at. It was also higher than they'd told me they were planning on spending.

I was now seriously concerned.

When we went through the numbers together, I showed them what I'd found around purchasing at the prices they'd previously talked about. Then I updated the numbers with the actual figures from their purchase … and we quickly realised some adjustments would be needed. I could see Anthony and Mia's stress levels rise.

They were both earning good money. Anthony was an executive for a big company and was well looked after, while Mia was being paid maternity leave and had a good job to return to. But they'd extended themselves so much on their high-priced property that the ongoing costs of the property and mortgage didn't leave much room in their budget for the other spending that was important to them.

Anthony was from the UK, Mia was a Kiwi, and they both had most of their family overseas. They loved to travel and had told me in the early stages of their planning that this was one of the most important things to factor into their spending plan. They also wanted to do some renovations to their new place to set it up the way they wanted it. But the position they'd put themselves in meant that now wasn't an option.

I worked with them to help them balance their budget in a sustainable way. But they weren't happy: their travel budget was cut, renovations were delayed, and their everyday spending also copped a big hit. Not only could they no longer spend the money they wanted, but they also had NO money left over for savings or paying down their debt.

And without a healthy pay rise, change of career or winning lotto, things didn't look any better for the next FIVE YEARS.

So where did Anthony and Mia go wrong? Apart from the obvious fact that they didn't finish their strategy before they executed on it, there was an underlying problem. And it's one I've seen before.

The real problem that caused them to move forward without making sure their strategy would work was their emotions. They'd let their emotions get involved and become the driving force behind their property purchase.

I understand that when you're thinking about buying a property, you can get caught up in the emotions of the purchase. You can't help but think about how the property 'feels' to you. If you're buying for your own home, you imagine yourself in there. You imagine your family in there. You start thinking about all the memories you'll create. Where you'll hang your pictures. What colour you'll paint the feature wall. What you'll look like sitting on the balcony 20 years from now, and what your life will look like.

Even if you're buying the property as an investment, you still think about whether you'd like to live in it, how it feels to you, whether the neighbours will be friendly or douchebags, etc. It's difficult to avoid. But it's possible.

Even though buying property can be an emotional decision, you need to understand at the end of the day that it's an investment. You're considering spending half a MILLION dollars or more, so it's most definitely an investment. Ask yourself how the most successful investors make their investment decisions. I'll give you a hint: they keep their emotions out of their purchase decisions.

And you need to do the same if you want to get the best money outcomes from your property purchase.

Now, if you're only concerned about the best emotional outcomes from your property purchase, you can ignore this. But if good financial outcomes and avoiding financial problems are also important, you need to learn from successful investors and not let emotions drive your choices.

Even though buying property can be an emotional decision, you need to understand at the end of the day that it's an investment.

Doing this is actually a fairly simple, three-step process (although not many people follow it):

1. Set your property strategy and understand the numbers.
2. Look at what properties fit into the strategy you've set.
3. Restrict your search to ONLY properties that fit within your strategy.

Your property purchase should be driven by the numbers: what you can afford, how much to borrow, and how to structure your purchase. ONLY once you're clear on your numbers should you start looking at the sorts of properties that fit into your strategy.

Simple, right? But so many people don't do this. Instead, they find properties they 'like' (or even worse, 'love'), and then try to make their strategy fit around the property. If you want to make the best decisions and avoid the trouble that Anthony and Mia experienced, remove your emotions from the property-buying process and set your strategy first.

How to create a cracking property strategy

When you're putting together a property purchase strategy, there are a few related steps you need to follow. The right property strategy for you will be almost entirely driven by your income, spending and savings position, so it's critical to get those right before you try to do any sort of planning around buying property. You can refer back to Chapter 5 for how to approach saving and spending.

And, as an extra note, I'd suggest having your system up and running for a minimum of three months before you buy property. This will give you confidence that your spending and saving plan works before you lock yourself into such a serious commitment.

The key elements of your strategy are as follows:

- How to structure your purchase.
- How much to spend and how much to borrow.
- How to structure your mortgage.
- How to manage your risk.
- How to understand your entry point.

I'm going to run through each of these areas below.

How to structure your purchase

When I refer to 'structuring' your purchase, the biggest factor is whether to buy your property as an investment or as your own home. What's best for you will depend on what's most important to you, but there's often a significant difference between the financial impact or 'cash flows' of these two options.

Most people don't give much thought to how they want to buy property. They might think about how much they hate their property manager or landlord. Maybe they think about whether they can afford the sort of property they want. Or perhaps, they just wish they could paint a feature wall the new caramel beige pecan colour they saw on their last trip to Bunnings.

Buying a property as your own home can be great. You get security. You can set the place up however you like. But in most cases, it's more expensive than buying property as an investment. This is because you need to pay your mortgage with after-tax dollars, and then have to pay all the ongoing costs of the property like strata, rates and maintenance. This restricts what you can afford, as well impacting your spending and saving capacity after your purchase.

Buying property as an investment doesn't have the same security benefits as buying for your own home. But it does give you some tax benefits, plus more flexibility around where you buy (because you don't have to want to live there) and the type and size of property (again because you don't have to live there). It also gives you the ability to live wherever you want depending on what's happening in your career and personal life.

Because of the tax benefits of buying an investment property, it's important to at least consider this as an option. If you dismiss it after working through the benefits and educating yourself, you've lost nothing other than a small amount of time. But what you'll gain is confidence that the strategy you've chosen is the best thing for you.

Note: There are also some other tricky options like buying through a trust or company. For the vast majority of property buyers though, these sort of structures are too complex and expensive to be justified.

Comparing structures

Meet Nick (not his real name), a creative professional who was renting a sweet converted warehouse apartment on Goulburn Street, Surry Hills. If you don't know the area, it's right on the fringe of the Sydney CBD, around 500m away from the centre of the city. Nick enjoyed this space, and felt comfortable unleashing his creative side there. It had a huge open-plan living area with his studio setup, which he also loved.

But he'd decided that the time had come to 'get his adult on' and buy property. He'd been saving for a while, and almost had enough for a deposit on a place. He was getting close to taking the leap and had started actually looking at properties.

When we got chatting, he told me that he was happy to be buying, but a little disappointed because he couldn't afford the type of property he wanted. He'd done some rough numbers and figured he'd need to move around 10 kilometres from the CBD. He didn't want to live that far from the city, but we both agreed that buying around Marrickville (a suburb about 8km from the Sydney CBD) would still be a solid investment that would increase well in value over time.

So we started looking at the numbers.

Before buying property (yearly figures)	
Income	$160 000
Tax	$39 000
Spending (excl. rent)	$61 000
Rent	$20 000
Net Savings	$40 000

Note: This is a very simplified part of the planning process, and is just for illustrative purposes. If you're planning around property, you'll need to go into more detail than just putting together these tables.

In our example, Nick was saving strongly at $40k each year, and he was thinking about spending around $700k on a property. Together, we looked at how this purchase might impact his financial position, depending on whether he bought for his own home, or as an investment.

Buying as own home (yearly figures)	
Income	$160 000
Tax	$39 000
Spending (excl. rent)	$61 000
Rent	–
Mortgage ($700k interest only @ 5%)	$35 000
Property costs, i.e. strata (@1%)	$7000
Net savings annually	$18 000

You can see a couple of changes in this scenario. We removed rent, because Nick is moving out of his rental apartment, and added in mortgage costs at a conservative interest rate of 5 per cent. We also included an allowance of 1 per cent for property-related costs like strata, rates, management costs and other related costs.

In this scenario, Nick is still saving $18 000 every year, but this is significantly less than his previous $40 000 p.a. This implies that the purchase costs him $22 000 net each year. The strategy 'works' though, in that it's possible for Nick to keep saving—so if he was happy with it, he could follow it. But he wasn't happy: he didn't want to move that far from the city. So we looked at an alternative.

The second scenario involved Nick buying the property as an investment, and continuing to rent the current place he loved. He preferred this scenario because it still got him into the property market, but also let him live where he wanted.

Buying investment property (yearly figures)	
Income	$160 000
Tax	$39 000
Spending (excl. rent)	$61 000
Rent	$20 000
Net savings annually (excluding property numbers below)	$40 000
Property cash flow	
Rental income (4%)	$28 000
Mortgage ($700k interest only @ 5%)	$35 000
Property costs, i.e. strata (@1%)	$7000
Property net cash flow	−$14 000
Tax refund (39% of net cost)	$5460
Investment property net cost after tax	−$8540
Overall Cash flow	
Nick's net savings annually (excluding property)	$40 000
Investment property net cost after tax	$8540
Overall cash flow (net savings annually)	$31 660

In this scenario, we again included rent, as well as the costs of buying the property. But Nick now has rental income from the new investment property he's bought. Plus he gets the tax impact of buying an investment property, where the net cost of holding the property provides a tax deduction. That means he receives a refund at his marginal tax rate (39 per cent in Nick's case).

In this scenario, the impact on Nick's savings and the total cost of the investment property is $8540, which is almost a third of the cost of buying as his own home ($22 000). In both scenarios, he buys the exact same property. The only difference is how he's structured his purchase. And the additional benefit of the second scenario is that he can continue living where he wants: an important lifestyle benefit for Nick.

Most people don't think in these terms though. I can't even count how many times I've heard the expressions 'paying rent is dead money' or 'I don't want to pay off someone else's mortgage'. These ideas have been conditioned into us by our parents and society, but that doesn't mean they're right.

Yes, if you just pay rent and waste the rest of your cash, it absolutely *is* dead money. But, if you instead choose to rent and then do something SMART with the money you've saved by renting, you can boost your money results. That was the case for Nick.

I'm not saying that buying property as an investment is the best decision for everyone. I'm *definitely* not saying it's the best decision for you. The difference in outcomes will depend on your situation, income, assets and strategy.

What I am saying is that you'll often get significantly different financial outcomes from buying the exact same property either as an investment, or as your own home. That's why I strongly believe you should take the time before you buy to understand what the difference would be for you specifically.

This will allow you to make the best decision for you, and do it fully informed and confident that you're making the right choice.

> **You'll often get significantly different financial outcomes from buying the exact same property either as an investment, or as your own home.**

How much to spend and how much to borrow

Buying and borrowing at different levels will have different impacts on how much you'll be able to spend, save or use for debt reduction following your purchase. If you don't think through this impact on your spending and saving, you can end up stuck in a position where you don't have enough money left over for the things that are important to you.

How to structure your mortgage

There are a stack of options for structuring your mortgage: interest only, principal and interest, variable, fixed, combination of variable and fixed, low-doc, lender choice, offset accounts, redraw and more. Each of these variables will impact your money position following your purchase and into the future. They'll also have a big impact on the two steps above, so it will pay to get your mortgage structure right.

Understand also that lending options are in constant flux, so there's no one 'best' structure option. The best option for you will depend on what you're trying to achieve with your property strategy, and the options available at the time you purchase. So ensure you get up-to-date lending options close to that time.

> Mortgage broking is a free service, as the broker is paid by the bank. The right person will help you create a better borrowing strategy—but you do need to find a good one. Ask someone with solid financial knowledge to recommend a professional they know who'll deliver the right outcome.

Risk Management

Risk management is a big part of the steps above. This involves looking at the numbers and financial impacts of buying property at different price points and borrowing levels, and with different property buying and borrowing structures. This then allows you to plan ahead, and will help you to feel comfortable with the financial outcomes you're working towards.

When you buy property, you'll probably depend mostly on your income (or two incomes if you're buying as a couple) to afford your mortgage payments. This means an important part of managing risk is protecting your income, which in turn means income replacement insurance (and life insurance for couples).

I strongly believe that it's crazy to buy a property without having this sort of insurance in place. I actually believe everyone should have income insurance whether they own property or not. I won't get into personal insurance in this book—mainly because it's insanely complicated and dry as cardboard—but look into this as part of your risk management strategy.

Pro Tip

When looking at the numbers for your property strategy, factor in an interest rate at least 2 per cent above the current one. This will build mortgage risk management into your strategy, and give you confidence that future changes won't catch you unprepared.

Understand your entry point

Going through the steps above should give you a good idea of how much you can spend and borrow. This allows you to understand how much money you'll need to get into the market, i.e. your deposit and the costs of buying property.

Remember: we said earlier that entry costs for Australian residential property average around 5 per cent of the purchase price, including stamp duty, legal fees, title searches, and other incidental costs. On top of this, you'll need a deposit—typically around 8-12 per cent of the property's value at the time I'm writing this.

Once you've set your property strategy, I want you to grab a piece of paper (or create a new document on your computer) and write down how much money you'll need to get started. Then grab your saving plan and calculate when you'll reach this savings target. Break it down into months, and add each date to your calendar. This will give your motivation a huge boost, and will reduce your chances of getting off track.

Why do this? Without a clear entry point, building your deposit will seem like an almost impossible task that will take forever. Clarifying that entry point will help you nail down *exactly* when it will all come together. Then, once your timeline is set, any misstep isn't just you giving into that desire to treat yourself to an afternoon at the spa, or a beard treatment. It's not just 'a weekend away that you desperately deserve because you work hard and work out five times a week and eat healthy and your boss is an asshole and YOU JUST DESERVE IT OKAY?'

Instead, it's a clear warning that you're moving further away from getting that property you really want. When you reframe your thinking in this way, you'll feel the pain of working outside your plan, and you're more likely to stay on track.

You can't understand your entry point without following all the steps above, but it *is* a critical step in the property purchasing process to give yourself the clarity and motivation you'll need to get what you want.

Family Guarantee

This strategy isn't for everyone, but if you're buying your first home, you need to understand it to know whether it might be right for you. Using it may give you a huge leg up in your property strategy, and get you what you want much sooner.

The strategy has many names: a family guarantee, equity guarantee, family pledge, guarantor, or a few other variations. Regardless though, the strategy is the same. It involves using the value of another property (often your parents' home) as an 'equity' guarantee for the deposit on the property you want to buy. Equity is just the difference between the value of a property and the amount of debt owing on its mortgage.

For example: if your family's home is worth $500k, and there's a mortgage on that property of $200k, the property's 'equity' is it value – debt (i.e. $500k – $200k = $300k).

Because banks understand property and are comfortable using either this or cash as security, they will normally lend you up to 80 per cent of a property's value secured against the 'equity'.

So for this strategy, the available equity = 80 per cent of the property value. That means that if the property you want is worth $500k, the available equity = 80 per cent of its value ($500k * 80 per cent = $400k).

And the amount the bank will comfortably lend against your property is equal to the available equity minus debt: in this case this, $400k – $200k = $200k.

Net result: if your folks are cool with this strategy and you want to borrow to buy your first home, the bank will give you up to $200k to use as your deposit. Even if you have enough money together for this deposit, you may not want to use it. You might want to ensure you've got some money aside for emergencies or unexpected expenses following your purchase.

It's worth noting that even with this strategy, you still need to be able to afford the mortgage. There are also other complex aspects that you need to understand. But if you *can* access this strategy, it can help you to get into the property market straight away, and keep your cash savings as your emergency fund.

IMPORTANT: because this gets quite technical, I won't go into any further detail here. If you'd like more information, you can refer to this video: bit .ly/GUStools

If you're thinking about using a family guarantee strategy it's essential to take the time to set a good overall financial strategy. Along with good insurance, a good strategy will manage almost all your risk and ensure your decisions don't create unnecessary risk for your parents.

Pro Tip

If you build out your property strategy and find that the only limiting factor is your deposit, go and buy your mum a present today.

Then chat to a mortgage or financial expert who understands this strategy, equip yourself with the knowledge you need, and ask your parents whether you can use the strategy to kick-start your property strategy.

Choosing the right property

It sounds like common sense, but the property you choose *will* dictate the returns you receive over time. And your expected return on that property should align with the level of risk involved in your investment.

In my financial advice business, we generally advise against chasing 'property hotspots', trying to pick the next big thing, or trying to read the future in tea leaves. When formulating your property investment strategy, instead choose quality properties that will remain in demand over time. These are more likely to benefit from strong long-term returns.

The two biggest factors that influence how a property's value grows over time is the demand from other buyers, and the level of supply, i.e. how many other properties are available to buy. If the property is in an area lots of people want to buy or live in (i.e. high demand) and there's little new land available for new properties (limited supply), its value will increase over time.

How supply and demand impact property values

To use a real-world example of how supply and demand impact property prices, let's look at the town of Moranbah, QLD. Moranbah is a small town around 1000 kilometres north of Brisbane. It's mainly a mining town because BHP Billiton (Australia's largest mining company) have a large coal mining operation not far away.

Around 2010 there was a huge mining boom in Australia. Coal around Australia sold at a very high price, so miners wanted to get it out of the ground as quickly as possible. BHP expanded their operations in Moranbah, and hired as quickly as they could to increase coal production. Some of my cousins are geologists in the mining industry, and they were posted to Moranbah at that time.

When they relocated, so many people were moving to Moranbah that it was hard for anyone to find a property to rent. So, as you'd expect, rental prices went through the roof. Another way of saying this is that there was huge demand and limited supply.

In 2002, before this mining boom, the median (or middle market) property price in Moranbah was $24 299 (yes, less than $25k). But the huge increase in demand combined with the limited property supply over the next ten years pushed the median property value up to $490 500.

During this time, many property investors were drawn to buy in Moranbah, chasing the rising prices and trying to make some quick money in the process. This pushed the property prices in the area even higher; and by the end of 2012, the average price in Moranbah was over $580k.

Then in 2012, the global prices for coal dropped, which led the big mining companies to wind back their operations in places like Moranbah. They stopped sending workers to the area, and started relocating workers from Moranbah to other more profitable areas. Fewer miners in Moranbah meant less demand for property, and the average property price dropped to below $240 000.

This is a reduction of over 50 per cent: a huge drop by any standard. And the property investors in Moranbah were suffering. I saw one story on the current affairs program 60 Minutes about a 24-year-old property investor who'd borrowed $6.5 million to buy 10 investment properties in Moranbah with the dream of retiring before 30.

Initially, she'd made millions as the prices rose, and at its peak her property portfolio was worth close to $10m. Once property values crashed though, she was in real trouble. At the time the story went to air, her properties were worth less than half of their purchase price — and half the amount she owed on them. She had to declare bankruptcy because she had no hope of recovering the $3m she'd lost.

Early in your money journey, it's hard to recover from this sort of setback. But was this investor unlucky, or was there more to it?

In reality, she'd bought these properties hoping to make some big money fast from the rapid price rises in the area. As we discussed in the last chapter on investing though, big returns (especially *fast*, big returns) involve more risk than steady, slower, long-term returns do.

It shouldn't have taken a genius to see that the mining boom wouldn't continue forever. So demand *would* eventually decline — and if long-term demand won't continue for any asset or investment, its value won't continue to increase.

What happened to this property investor (and others in Moranbah) was unfortunate. At the same time, though, they were trying to make fast money through investing in something that didn't have a solid foundation. They let greed get in the way of common sense and good judgement — and they paid the price.

Stick to the fundamentals when you buy property to avoid this sort of trouble.

What returns do you need?

When buying property, refer back to your planning. Think through how much you need to make from your property investment to get the money outcomes you want over time. We've discussed that with any investing, it's natural to want to make as much money as possible, but remember: you don't need to shoot the lights out. And when you buy property, the higher the return you're chasing, the more risk there will be in your investment.

Yes, you could try your luck picking the next property hotspot. You could source the best new 'sure thing' property investment strategy online, or follow the buy/reno/flip property strategy in an attempt to make more money faster. These strategies can sometimes work, but they also generally involve higher levels of risk.

If, on the other hand, you take the time to plot out a solid, long-term strategy for your money that includes property, you probably won't need these higher risk levels to get the money results you want over time.

So what DO you look for? When I advise my clients, I generally recommend purchasing in areas with strong projected population growth. You can access this information on the Australian Bureau of Statistics (ABS) website: www.abs.gov.au/. This will help you to figure out where future demand will increase long-term property values. In practice, this generally means buying good properties in 'blue-chip' areas, which have the added advantage of less land being available for new developments (i.e. limited supply).

In regional or rural areas, there's a lot of land available. Drive a few hours from a major city, and you'll see that properties become more spread out. If you're buying in an area where there's a huge amount of land, you have to ask yourself why someone would pay more for your property later on if they can just go a few kilometres down the road to a huge block of land that 10/20/50 houses could be built on.

> **Keeping supply and demand front of mind as you buy will help you choose a property that will generate stable long-term growth.**

Keeping supply and demand front of mind as you buy will help you choose a property that will generate stable long-term growth.

Another significant factor in a property purchase is land value, which will drive the increase in your property price over time. Once you're comfortable with the area you're looking to buy in, I typically suggest trying to purchase as much land as possible.

Suburbs in Australia and around the world are increasing in density. Houses are being replaced by townhouses, which are being replaced by apartments, which are in turn being replaced by larger and larger apartment developments. When you buy property, it's actually the land that drives the growth in property value over time.

A house on a block of land is a good option because you're the only owner of the land under your property. This might not be realistic for you: houses are becoming more and more expensive. Still, if you're looking to buy an apartment, try to maximise the amount of land you get. A smaller block of apartments will mean you own a greater share of the land than a big apartment block. If you buy in a block of 50 apartments, you'll only own 2 per cent of the total land, but if you own an apartment in a five-unit block, you'll own 20 per cent of the land.

Keep this in mind when you're shopping around and try to get the *maximum* land exposure possible from your investment.

The future of property

In most western countries, buying property has historically been a great way to make money. House prices in Australia have doubled in pretty much every ten-year period since federation. Many people in older generations (including most of our parents) have made good money buying property.

But the way we live and work is changing due to better technology and faster and faster internet speeds, and I believe this trend will continue. Today you can work from anywhere. This book was written across seven countries on four continents (I may even squeeze in a fifth before the final edit is complete). Most of my mates and clients work at least one day from home, and I've noticed this trend increasing significantly in the last couple of years.

Most organisations realise the traditional office is an expensive and unproductive way to manage a workforce. I read a couple of great articles on Inc.com and News.com the other day that both estimated the average office-based workday for most people consists of around three fully productive hours. So why would companies continue to force their staff to sit in an expensive central office when they'd be happier and more efficient working from home or satellite offices? (And it would be cheaper that way too.)

Let me ask you a question. If you could live and work from anywhere, where would it be? Would you choose where you are right now, or would you rather be on a beach somewhere — perhaps Byron, Malaga, the South of France or Rio de Janeiro?

I'd love to move out of the city at some point, but for now I'm happy living in Glebe, just a couple of kilometres from Sydney. I think that if everyone could live anywhere, a bunch of people would still want to live in Glebe. We've got good cafes. It's close to everything. There are plenty of good restaurants. And it's pretty peaceful.

I can say the same thing about virtually all suburbs within five kilometres of Sydney's CBD, and most other capital cities on the East Coast of Australia. But I can't say the same about the outer suburbs of Sydney, where average property prices are over $1m, you need a huge mortgage to buy into the market, and traffic is terrible.

Personally, I'd rather spend less money buying a home on the beach close to Byron, the Spanish coast, Ecuador or Bali. Would everyone do this? No. But would a few? I think yes. Maybe more than a few. There are some beautiful places in Australia and around the world that are very cheap to live. Could you imagine people being happy to move if it meant they saved hundreds of thousands of dollars and increased their financial security?

This, of course, impacts demand. The more people who move out of major cities and typical suburban areas, the less demand will exist for properties in those areas. No doubt this will impact how quickly property values grow over time. If you buy property expecting values to increase at the same rate over the next 50 years that they have in the last 50 years, I think you could be in for a surprise.

I believe these factors mean buying property today carries more risk than investing in other assets like the share market. No matter how much where we live and work changes, I can't see there ever being a time where smart companies who run good businesses don't make money. This tells me the share market is more likely to continue to generate good returns for investors over time.

Now I'm not a property expert. Or a sociology expert. I could be completely wrong about all of this. But I can see the trends changing the way people work, and I think this will have an impact on how and where we live.

I don't think property values will stop increasing, or that there will be a dramatic crash. People always want *somewhere* to live. I don't believe property values will increase at the same rate they've done in the past though. So that means that buying property anywhere further than five kilometres away from a major city involves risk.

And that, in turn, means it's more important than ever to be strategic about how, where and why you buy property.

PUTTING IT ALL TOGETHER

This chapter on property is the biggest in this book for good reason. Buying property is one of the biggest financial decisions and commitments you'll make. It's also extremely complex, and there are many things to consider to get your property strategy right.

The consequences of getting your strategy wrong are severe, and can cause difficulties in your money strategy for many years. Unfortunately, I've seen too many people who've rushed into buying property without thinking through all the points above and paid the price.

I passionately believe that nobody should have to suffer through this. But there's so much misinformation and bad advice, and so many bad ideas around property that it's often hard to cut through the noise. I hope this chapter helps you get started on building a solid strategy for yourself.

Buying property involves several steps that are all linked together. Each one is important, and if you get them all right you'll end up with a great property strategy that will give you benefits for years to come. I've only been able to scratch the surface of the complex layers of these steps in this chapter, but you can address each step using the planning process we covered in the last section.

One final suggestion: if you're not a property, finance or mortgage expert, seek out someone who is to get the best results from your property purchase. You're talking about spending significant money, so a good professional (or team of professionals) will pay for themselves *many* times over.

CHAPTER 12

Don't be old and poor

Human beings are generally pretty bad at thinking ahead. It's our nature to care more about our immediate satisfaction and happiness than about making sacrifices for a benefit at some vague point in the distant future. This means we're likely to delay making difficult choices that we know we should probably think about, but aren't ready to take action on just yet.

I was recently reading about why this is, and found that one of the key drivers of 'short termism' is how difficult we find it to imagine what our future selves will want. The longer the period in question, the more difficult it is to identify with our future selves. So if you're thinking about what to have for lunch this Friday, you'll probably have a pretty good idea. But trying to imagine what you'll want for lunch 20 years from today is much more difficult.

Adding in the requirement to sacrifice something now makes it even harder. For example, being more health-conscious will make your future self healthier, happier and probably sexier. But it means you have to put in the hours at the gym, sacrifice leisure time and say no to some stuff now.

And it's the same with money. Building your savings, investments and assets will make your future self more financially secure and can create a better lifestyle many years from now. It may even potentially allow you to retire early. But it involves putting in work now to save money and say no to things you want. It means not going away with your partner or mates to your favourite weekend getaway spot. It means turning down that extra special dinner at the hottest new restaurant in town, or not buying that extra stylish pocket square or clutch from your favourite fashion boutique.

Your future self won't have lower expectations than you do.

I know: you want satisfaction. You don't want to sacrifice. And while you probably can't even picture your future self, **you should recognise the fact that future-you won't be massively different to current-you.** You want to enjoy your life every day and be able to live well. So does your future self. You enjoy treating yourself with some of the good things in life. That won't change either. Your future self won't have lower expectations than you do.

Important things aren't urgent *unless* they're neglected

If you're like most people I meet, you have big hopes and expectations for your future. You work hard trying to set up a life for yourself, and expect to enjoy the benefits of this hard work in the future. You want to be able to help family and the people and causes you care about.

But imagine working through your entire career, just to reach a point where you have to LOWER your expectations and settle for a standard of living that's less than you're used to. This isn't my idea of a life well lived. Is it yours?

Most people don't start looking at their super until they get close to retirement. I've seen this happen. In my first job in the financial advice world, I met countless people in their 50s who'd neglected their long-term savings for most of their working life. They knew they should have been doing something much earlier. Instead, they fell into the trap of prioritising things that seemed urgent but weren't as important, instead of things (like securing their retirement savings) that weren't urgent but WERE very important.

Recently released figures based on the Australian national savings rate (cited on AMPCapital.com) of 4.7 per cent show that the average 30-year-old in Australia today faces the prospect of retiring at age 60 on $65 000 p.a.

This may sound okay until you realise that rising prices and income levels over this period mean that $65k p.a. will only equate to 27 per cent of the average Australian income in 30 years' time (the equivalent of about $28k of income today).

Here are the numbers:

- The average super balance for a 30-year-old in Australia is currently $38 861, while the average full-time income is $98 218, and standard super contributions are 11.5% (based on statistics cited in a 2021 ASFA report and 2023 ABS income data).
- Based on a 3% income growth rate across the country, that average income is projected to grow to over $238k in 30 years.
- Based on long-term investment performance figures and super tax (discussed below), that average super balance would grow to $1 305 736 over 30 years.
- Based on 5% annual income, that future super would generate an income of $65 269 each year, which is only 27% of the average $238k income.
- Further, that $65k is in FUTURE dollars where everything will cost more. Based on an inflation rate of 3%, this $65k would be worth only $28 123 in TODAY dollars.

What sort of future life do you want?

Relying on 27 per cent of the average income in the future would make it pretty difficult to look after yourself, let alone anyone else.

Your ability to live the life you imagined when you were young would go out the window.

Helping out your loved ones would need to be scrapped.

Date nights with your partner? Out the window too.

And travelling regularly would be almost impossible.

If you want to live well in the future, you need to acknowledge that future-you won't want to make these huge sacrifices. You'll want to live at a standard that's at least as good as today's, and ideally better.

But acknowledging it isn't enough. You actually need to do something more than just crossing your fingers and hoping that blind optimism will somehow boost your future bank balance.

> **You need to do something more than just crossing your fingers and hoping that blind optimism will boost your future bank balance.**

Trust me. It won't.

The good news is that there's hope. If you invest, starting small and being consistent will build steady momentum and lead to great outcomes.

For example, extra contributions to your super fund of less than $23 per day will grow your fund by an extra $1.23m by the time you reach age 60. That's barely the cost of lunch with your mates or a cocktail at your favourite after-work watering hole.

And this additional super money would more than double your retirement income to just over $126k p.a. in future dollars. This would bring you to 53 per cent of the national average income at that time, which is a pretty solid improvement. Obviously the more you can put in each month, the more freedom future-you will have to enjoy life without money getting in the way.

Before you dismiss this idea saying you can't afford $23 a day (or $690 per month), consider how quickly you're likely to adjust to any change in your situation.

Imagine you received a pay rise of $690 per month: I bet you'd feel great. In the first month afterwards, you'd notice this extra cash in your account. And maybe you would in the second month, too, but you'd quickly find something to spend (or waste) it on. Then you'd quickly adjust, and soon wouldn't even notice the extra money. It wouldn't significantly change your life.

In the same way, if you took a pay cut of $690 per month, the adjustment would be just as quick. Your life wouldn't change much (if at all).

Long story short? Just make it happen. You won't even notice the money is missing in a few months, but future-you will thank you for it.

This is a simple example, but there are several important rules you need to think about before you rush out and start cranking up your super fund contributions. Depending on what's important to you right now, other actions might be more effective than building your super.

Pro Tip

Get personalised advice and understand the rules in detail before you take action. For now, just understand the power and results you can create by starting small and building your momentum steadily over time.

The key is that whatever you do, you NEED to get started. The sooner you get started, the easier it is to get results and the less you'll feel the pinch of having to save. Don't bury your head in the sand and think you can just solve this problem later, or you'll pay a heavy price. Set your super strategy now, and be consistent so you can give your future self the epic lifestyle you deserve.

> **The sooner you get started, the easier it is to get results and the less you'll feel the pinch of having to save.**

We've already seen that starting small, being consistent, and building on your momentum can lead to great financial results. And when it comes to your superannuation or retirement fund, things get even better because of the favourable tax treatment given to super funds.

Super fund tax

The Australian government created the superannuation retirement savings (super) scheme to help people save money. They didn't create it because they're just good people who want to look after you. Instead, they want you to save so they don't have to fund your retirement through government benefits.

To encourage you to save enough to fund your retirement, they offer tax incentives for contributing money to your super account. They do this in a couple of ways. Firstly, the tax rate on any investment earnings your super fund generates is lower than your standard marginal tax rate. And secondly, you get a tax deduction for making contributions to your super fund.

Tax on investment income

As we covered in Chapter 9, if you invest in your personal name, you pay tax on any investment income at your marginal tax rate. In comparison, your earnings on your super fund are taxed at a maximum rate of 15 per cent.

Remember that if you earn more than \$45000 p.a., your marginal tax rate is at least 32 per cent. This means that if you earned \$10000 of investment income each year in your personal name, you'd pay tax of \$3200. But if you generated an investment income of \$10000 each year in your super fund, you'd only pay tax of \$1500.

This represents a tax saving of \$1700 EVERY SINGLE YEAR.

And because this tax saving stays in your super fund and is reinvested with your other super money, it has the compounding effect that's so beautiful with investments. Your investments and assets will grow faster, and you'll make more progress setting yourself up for the future.

Tax on contributions to super

And making extra contributions to super is just as good. You can contribute personally to your super fund before tax up to a limit (currently \$30000 each year).

These contributions are deducted from your income *before* your tax is calculated. This means you don't pay income tax on this money, which results in an immediate tax benefit to you personally. The money you would have paid out in tax is instead directed to your super fund where it can work for you, instead of just being dead money paid to the tax office to fund some politician's fancy lunch at the Canberra Shangri La.

These contributions *are* taxed by your super fund at 15 per cent when they're received. But again, the difference between this rate and your marginal tax rate is a direct tax saving for you. **So as with the example above, if you contributed \$10000 to your super fund pre-tax, you'd be directly saving \$1700 in tax.**

Both of the examples above are based on a relatively low income. If your income was higher, your tax savings would be even greater.

A word of warning though: all these tax breaks are great, but it's also important to consider your personal strategy for building investment assets outside of super.

Once you put money into super, it's effectively 'trapped' until you reach age 60 (under current rules). And because the government has a tendency to change the rules around super, you need a backup strategy. If they were to extend the age for accessing your super even further, you'd need access to other investments unless you're happy working full-time until retirement age.

How to live like a rockstar in the future

If you don't have a strategy to grow your retirement savings beyond what you'll receive from the government, you're headed for a bleak retirement. And you don't want to put in the hard yards through your working life just to deliver your future self a life you don't love.

The good news is that setting a good strategy then starting small and being consistent makes it much easier to fill this gap. Here's an example of how extra contributions to your super fund at different levels will help grow your savings faster.

Contribution Level	Percentage of Average Wage (age 60 retirement)
11.5% contributions (compulsory only)	27%
Additional 3% contributions	34%
Additional 6% contributions	40%
Additional 9.5% contributions	48%
Additional 15.5% contributions	56%

You can see from the table above that if you could manage to contribute an additional 15.5 per cent of your income to your Super, you'd get a huge boost to your retirement income. You'd go from just 27 per cent of the average future income from compulsory contributions alone to more than doubling that result and retiring on 56 per cent of the average income.

And it gets better.

As we covered above, you can contribute to your super fund BEFORE tax. This means that you don't even have to pay the full cost of making these contributions.

Let's jump into the numbers again:

- The current average income is $98 218 p.a.
- Assuming you were paid this average, 15.5% of your income would equate to $15 224 p.a.
- Because you make your super contributions pre-tax, the reduction in your AFTER-TAX pay is the full amount less the tax (at least 32% assuming income above $45 000).
- After-tax costs = total amount ($15 224) – tax you would have paid ($4871) or $10 352 ($15 224 – $4871).
- Breaking down this annual super contribution of $10 352 equates to $28.36 daily (=$10 352 /365).

The benefit here is that your extra super contributions are coming from your pay BEFORE tax is applied. That means the cost you actually *feel* is lower because you'd have to pay tax on this money if you'd received it as income.

You might think that you couldn't afford to contribute to your super at this level. And I know this sounds corny, but can you afford not to?

These figures show that steadily making relatively small investments over time will make a huge difference to the outcomes you'll experience in the future. And if you want to create options for yourself and keep living the lifestyle you want, you need to think about this now.

The time to act is now. Any delay only means you'll have to sacrifice more in the future. You'll either have to put in much more of your own money, or you won't get to the same retirement income you otherwise would have.

For example, imagine that you choose to coast through your 30s and don't worry about putting any extra money aside. Then, in your 40s, you decide to start contributing an extra 15.5 per cent of your salary to your super. In this situation, your super balance will only give you 42 per cent of the average income (compared to the 56 per cent you'd get if you'd started at age 30). And if you wait until you're 50 to get started, you'll retire on 33 per cent of the average income. Like we covered in the previous chapter on investments, building initial momentum makes a huge difference.

And, as we saw in the same chapter, starting small and being consistent will deliver powerful results. But you do need to get started: remember that the best time to start was 20 years ago, and the second best time is right now. Set your super strategy now, and be consistent so you can deliver your future self the epic lifestyle you deserve.

The section above was all about the importance of having a strategy around your super fund that will allow you to create the future lifestyle you want. But I also want to tell you what you need to know to choose the *right* retirement savings account for you.

How to choose a super fund

So now that you know about the key areas and issues to be aware of around super, how do you choose the right fund for you? I've included a quick summary below to help you choose.

The right type of fund

The first thing you need to do is choose the type of fund you want to use, i.e. industry fund, retail, corporate (if available) or SMSF. I talk about each of these fund types and their features later on in this chapter.

Once you understand the differences, consider the features that are most important to you in a fund, and choose one that will give you these.

Investments that align with your strategy

This one should go without saying but it confuses many people. We talked about passive and active investment strategies back in Chapter 10. And if you want to follow a particular investment strategy, you need to use a fund that provides access to the investments you want.

When I'm advising clients, I typically recommend a passive investment approach using index funds. So when I help my clients to choose the right super fund for them, I look for a fund that allows access to passive investments. Similarly, clients who want to invest ethically need to use a super fund that gives access to ethical investment options.

Set your investment strategy first, then find the right super fund that will allow you to access the investments you want to use. This follows the planning framework we've covered through this book. Your strategy should always come *before* you choose solutions to support it.

Value-for-money fees

Fees definitely aren't everything when you're choosing a super fund. There are some very cheap funds that are garbage and some that are great, and the same goes with more expensive funds. I've met many people who think they need to get the cheapest possible super fund, but then don't pay attention to the quality of the product they get. You can't pay for silver and get gold. The key is getting value for money.

> **You can't pay silver and get gold. The key is getting value for money.**

If you're paying higher fees for access to more investments or additional features, take advantage of these benefits to ensure your money is well spent. That being said, if you're just getting started and your super balance is low, consider using a low-fee super fund to allow your money to grow faster.

Key super mistakes

There are some confusing rules around super funds and how they run. If you don't understand these rules, you can easily get caught out. Below are some of the common mistakes people make with super.

Automatic insurance cover

Most people don't realise that when they start a new fund, it often comes with automatic insurance cover, which is charged to the fund. Insurance is important to manage risk, but this automatic insurance can be a hidden cost that slows down the fund's growth.

It's also important to realise that the automatic insurance for some funds is more expensive than for others, and it's often not very good quality. If you have multiple super funds, they may all have insurance in the accounts you are paying for.

What you need to do: Take the time to understand how much insurance you need to cover your key risks. Then learn about your insurance options both within your current super funds and with other types of super policies.

You should probably have some insurance cover, but you need to understand what cover you have and what you're paying for it, so you can make an informed choice about whether it's right for you.

Note: I've said previously that I believe personal insurance like income replacement, disability and life insurance is super important. But it's not covered in this book, mainly because it's complicated AF and dry as cardboard. I still suggest you educate yourself about how it works and your options, though, to decide what's right for you.

Consolidating is important

If you've accumulated more than one super fund over the years through different employers, you're not alone. This doesn't seem like a big deal, but it can result in poor performance due to the different fees on multiple super funds.

Each super fund typically has a fixed fee built into its fee structure. So if you have more than one fund, you're paying more than one set of fees. We also talked about automatic insurance cover in each of your accounts above. If you have multiple insurance premiums coming from different accounts, it can end up impacting your money.

What you need to do: Take the time to explore and figure out which super fund is right for you. Then consolidate ALL your super money into this fund.

Pro Tip

Think about the insurance cover you have in your accounts when changing funds. Make sure you don't exit a super fund and lose the insurance cover in the account without replacing it.

Don't be over-conservative

When you don't have a strong understanding of investments, it's natural to want to minimise risk in your super fund. But there's good risk and bad risk, and understanding the difference will allow you to make smart choices with your super investments. Remember: a small difference in your return will make a big difference over time.

I've talked to many young professionals who view themselves as conservative investors. Once they understand how investments work and what this means for them though, they often realise that a more growth-focused portfolio suits them and their investment objectives better.

What you need to do: Educate yourself about investments so you can confidently set up a portfolio with the right amount of 'good' risk to get you the investment outcomes you want. Don't just stick to a conservative strategy because you haven't taken the time to fully understand the rules of the game.

Types of super funds

There are four main categories of the most common super funds available in Australia. I've put together a quick summary of each of these below, as well as key things to note about each type of fund.

Industry super funds

These are generally lower-cost, 'no frills' super funds. They typically have limited investment options, and most of the options are managed and administered by the super fund itself. The cost of these funds is normally between 0.5-1.5 per cent p.a.

What to look for: The low fees on these accounts mean they can be a good fund when you're just starting to grow your super. On the downside, their often-limited options can reduce flexibility when it comes to deciding what sort of investment strategy you want to follow.

Retail super funds

These funds are generally more expensive than industry funds, with costs typically running between 1-4 per cent p.a. They normally provide more investment options, detailed reporting and the ability to nominate an adviser on the account to assist with the ongoing management. The retail super fund space is very competitive, and funds are getting cheaper and better every year. So if you're using this type of fund, you should check in at least once a year to ensure your current fund is still the best one for you

Retail funds also often allow you to link your account to a Financial Adviser or advice company that can help manage and advise on the accounts.

What to look for: Cost isn't the most important factor when choosing a super fund, but you should be aware of the fees you're paying and ensure you're getting value for them.

Also as a side note on retail funds, I think most people have seen the TV ads comparing industry funds vs retail funds. These ads claim that industry funds are better because they're cheaper, so using an industry fund will mean you end up with more money at retirement.

In my opinion, these ads are misleading because they only look at fees. The truth is that if you use a fund that costs more but earns you more, you might be better off over time. Don't let this spin mislead you: make the right choice for *you* by informing yourself and understanding the options for your funds.

I've found that in many cases, retail funds can be a good option for growing your super over time because they give you access to a larger (and often higher quality) range of investment options.

Corporate funds

These are funds that are linked to your employer via a group deal with the super fund. This deal might result in lower fees and either discounted—or even free—insurance cover.

What to look for: Some of these funds are good, but others aren't. This means you need to look at the detail, and might even benefit from getting advice on your fund. Most of these corporate deals include a dedicated representative from the super fund company to answer your questions about the fund, so use this resource.

One big downside of corporate funds is that if you leave your employer, you'll often lose any discounts. This means your fees can jump up significantly. I've met a bunch of people who've been caught out by this trap, and have taken years after they left an employer to realise they were paying huge fees and not getting value from their ex-corporate super fund.

Self-managed superannuation funds (SMSF)

These funds provide a high degree of control over your fund management and access to virtually unlimited investment options, including residential and commercial properties. These funds are run like a company in that you need to do a tax return and other admin processes for them each year. This means they can be more expensive than other fund types.

What to look for: These funds can be great, but do involve a number of fixed costs that mean they're often not suitable unless you have at least $200000 in your super fund. The rules for these funds are also fairly complex, so if you want to use this sort of fund you'll probably need some good help in the form of an accountant, adviser, super fund administration provider, or all three.

PUTTING IT ALL TOGETHER

Most people tend to bury their heads in the sand when it comes to super. They put off thinking about their retirement savings and add it to their to-do list for a tomorrow that never comes.

They don't take the time to understand the importance of retirement savings or of putting a strategy in place to get their savings to the point they'll need to live the lifestyle they want. They also don't take the time to understand the rules and how they can get these rules working for them (and not just for their super company). On top of this, they ignore their own money sitting in an account, and don't bother choosing the right type of account or getting their investments in that account set up for what they want to achieve.

Please don't let this be you.

Hopefully this chapter has helped to bust a few myths and explained how to get your super working for you. If you take one thing from the chapter, it's to invest the time you need to understand the likely outcomes of following your current super strategy.

Then ask yourself whether you're happy with these results. If the answer is no, do something about it. *Now.* The sooner you take action, the smaller this action will need to be and the less you'll 'feel' it. Start building your momentum sooner and you'll make steady, consistent progress and reap huge benefits when it counts.

Do your future-self a solid and get started now.

CHAPTER 13

Reality, roadblocks and results

By now you should have a bunch of great ideas about what you can do to get better results from your money. But I want this book to be about *more* than ideas. I want it to be about action. All the learning in the world is useless without action to back it up.

Now it's time for the rubber to hit the road. It's time to do something practical with everything you've read, and time to put all the theory I've outlined in the book to use. Below you'll find an exercise I use with my financial advice clients that will help you get started on your path to money success. It steps you through exactly HOW to use the knowledge in this book to successfully set up your money strategy.

This exercise will help you get crystal clear on where you're at now, what's important to you, the results you want to achieve, and what's standing in your way. This will make it clear exactly where you should start and what to do next. I call the exercise the 'Three Rs', which stands for **Reality, Roadblocks** and **Results**.

The Three Rs exercise will help you get laser-focused on what success with money looks like to you, i.e. your Results. Then you'll get honest about where you are today, i.e. your Reality. And finally (but most importantly), you'll clarify what's standing between where you are now and where you want to be, i.e. your Roadblocks.

The Roadblocks section is the most important step, because it helps you to uncover whatever's holding you back. These roadblocks stand in the way of achieving the results you want with money. They'll become your list of action items, because if you can bust through and clear them, you'll be on the fast track to getting the money results you want.

To get the most out of the exercise, though, you'll need to do it in a roundabout way. I'll step you through this in detail so you know what to do. Start by drawing up the table shown below, or download the PDF I set up: bit.ly/GUStools.

YOUR ACTION PLAN

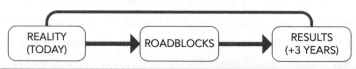

WHERE ARE YOU NOW?	WHAT'S IN THE WAY?	WHERE DO YOU WANT TO BE?
	Roadblocks, frustrations, problems, limitations, beliefs, fears, etc.	
Specific Goals		Specific Goals
Structure		Structure
Strategy		Strategy
Solutions		Solutions

Step 1—Results

We want to start this exercise at the end point you want to reach, which is the money results you want. Beginning here means you can dream big and list out all the things you want to get out of your money.

To start, I want you to imagine that we're sitting down together for a chat three years from today. You excitedly tell me, 'Ben, I'm completely blown away by the results I'm getting. I couldn't be happier with how things are going with my money strategy. I didn't even think it was possible for everything to go this well. I'm completely stoked!'

Now I want you to ask yourself what your situation actually looks like.

Think about what exactly is making you so happy about your progress. In particular, think about four key areas:

- Your specific goals.
- Your money management structure.
- Your broader strategy.
- Your goals around investment and product solutions.

I'll guide you through each of these areas, and give you some common examples of results that other people have come up with to help you get started. Please realise that there are no right or wrong answers here though. This is all on you. Success will probably mean something different to you than to most people, so dream big and think about what YOU want.

What specific results do you want?

The first area I want you to think about is your specific money or lifestyle wants.

Anything is on the table here, but you do need to be specific. This isn't about broader goals like 'having your money sorted' or 'having a really clear money strategy'. Instead, it's the specific things that are important to you.

Again, your answers depend entirely on what you care most about, but here are some common 'wants' I've seen to get you thinking:

- I want to have purchased my first home.
- I want to have an investment account worth $50k.
- I want to be completely debt free.
- I want to have three months' salary in cash savings for emergencies/my rainy day fund.
- I want to have taken that big trip to South America I've been planning for years.
- I want to start a family and take xxx months out of the workforce.
- I want to have started my own business.

The sky's the limit here, so include *anything* that's important to you. You need to be realistic, but don't worry about how you'll make it happen at this stage. Include all your specific goals in the 'Results' column in the box labelled 'Specific Goals'.

Now, we need to review your wants in relation to the three sections I've covered in this book: your money structure, strategy and solutions.

Structure

Remember that your money structure will drive how your money works on a day-to-day basis. When you think through the structure you want, consider how you'd like your money management to run. One of the critical objectives is setting up your finances to make it easy to get the results you want.

Common wants for money structure include:

- Knowing where your money is going, making sure you're getting real value/happiness for your spending, and stopping any unconscious spending or leakage.
- Putting a structure or process in place to automate your money management and make it easier to get the money outcomes you want.
- Getting clear on what money you have to work with so you can make smarter choices around your broader strategy and investments.
- Creating a structure for your money management that uses your money psychology and decision-making to work for you, instead of against you.
- Having an automated saving, spending and banking system.
- Having an automated investment system.
- Having an automated debt-reduction system.

Again, this is all driven by what's most important to you, so list out all your structure wants on your worksheet.

Strategy

The next area to look at is your strategy. Here, I want you to think about what you'd like your strategy to look like three years from today. This will depend on where you're at today, but think about how you want to improve your overall strategy.

Some common 'wants' that fall into the strategy area include:

- Understanding the money and/or lifestyle outcomes you're heading toward, i.e. having clear targets and goals, and a timeline for when you'll reach them.
- Knowing you've thought through all those outcomes, and that you've wrapped them into an overall strategy.

- Knowing that all the areas of your money are working together and heading in the same direction.
- Being clear on where your money is going.
- Having a clear strategy that prioritises everything that's important to you.
- Having a strategy that covers and manages your key risks.
- Knowing you're confidently taking action to follow your strategy.

Again, these are just a starting point, and some of them won't apply to you. So think through all the things that are important to you in relation to your overall strategy, and list them in the Results column in the box labelled 'Strategy'.

Solutions

Your solutions are the products and investments that support your strategy and drive your progress towards the results you want. You need to set up solutions that align with your strategy and structure for how you want to make money over time.

Common solutions wants include:

- Investment solutions that get your savings working harder for you and are set to make solid progress long-term.
- Knowing that these investments are consistent with your overall strategy and the plan you've set.
- An investment strategy that's set up to deliver reliable results over time, rather than chasing big money fast and running more risk than you need to get the results you want.
- Knowing your superannuation/retirement savings will drive the longer-term results you want.
- Knowing you have a solid safety buffer/security blanket in the form of cash to underpin your other investments.

Write a list of the results you want to get from your money strategy, so you can feel clear on what 'success' looks like to you. Once you know what your version of success is, you're much better placed to seek it out.

And, even more importantly, you'll know it when you get there.

Step 2—Reality

Next we're going to look at the 'Reality' column in the worksheet. This is a snapshot of where you're at today, so it *should* be the easy part. Your reality should also reference the results you want to get. In other words, if you listed a want in the Results section, your reality should relate back to this want.

For example, let's say you wrote 'Buy my first property' as a result you wanted. In the Reality section, you might list 'No property investments yet' or 'I don't know how much I need to buy property'. Or, you might have written 'Have an automated system for managing my savings and spending' as your result. In the Reality section for this, you might include 'No system for my spending and saving' or even 'No idea where my money goes or how best to manage it'.

The important thing is that each reality point you list should relate directly to a result you want. List out each of your reality points in the worksheet, and **align each one to the result it relates to**. Go through each of the results you want to achieve in the Specific Goals, Structure, Strategy and Solutions sections, and include your reality right now for each one.

Step 3—Roadblocks

This is by far the most important column. Your roadblocks are anything that stands between your reality (where you are now) and your results (what you want).

They're the most important because they'll become your list of action items once the exercise is complete. Clearing this list will move you from your current reality to the results you want.

It's CRITICAL to take the time to focus in detail on your true roadblocks. The more you put into this step, the easier your next steps will be. I'll do my best to give you some solid pointers, but I don't want you to gloss over this section. And be honest with yourself here: this list is for your eyes only.

Again, your roadblocks should align with the points you've included in your reality and results. Let's go back to the examples I listed in the Reality section above.

If the result you wanted was 'Buy my first property' and your reality was 'No property investments yet', your roadblocks might include 'I'm not clear on exactly how much I need as a deposit'. They might also include 'I'm not 100 per cent confident my property strategy is right for me' or 'I'm not good at saving'. Or it could be some combination of the three.

In the second example, the result you wanted was to 'Have an automated system to manage my saving and spending' and your reality was 'No system for either'. In this case, your roadblocks might be 'I'm not sure how to get started' or 'I don't know how to set up this system' or both.

Your roadblocks need to be more detailed than just 'I don't know what to do' or 'I don't have enough money'. They need to be higher-level obstacles that are the real cause of the issue. A good way to approach this whenever you come up with a roadblock is to ask yourself, 'Is there something else that's causing this problem?'

For example, if your initial roadblock is 'I don't have enough money', ask yourself what other issue could be causing this. It might be something like 'I don't have a plan around my saving and spending', 'I don't know where my money goes', or 'I don't have a system that makes it easy to save'. The differences between these can be subtle, but the impact is huge.

To figure out your roadblocks, look at a specific result on your list and ask yourself:

- Do I know what I need to do?
- Do I know the steps or process involved and where to start?
- Do I know the common mistakes to avoid?

If you can't answer yes to any of the questions, you need to list this as a roadblock.

Because this step is so important, I've made a longer list of prompts for you. The biggest and most common roadblocks for my clients are:

- being confused or overwhelmed with all the options and choices
- not being clear on all the rules or how to make them work for you
- not knowing the best approach to take to get started, and the best next steps to take
- not knowing how to create a strategy that will balance your money and lifestyle wants
- not knowing enough about the rules or things to consider to confidently take action
- not being sure how to set up a solid structure or system to support your strategy
- not knowing how to choose the right solutions to support your strategy
- not having enough time or knowledge to do this all yourself
- needing someone to push you and keep you accountable
- suffering from inaction (or maybe even procrastination) generally
- worrying that you might be missing something that will cause you to make mistakes.

Once you've listed your roadblocks, check that you haven't missed anything. You can do this by asking yourself whether clearing each roadblock is all you need to do to get to the result you want.

For example, let's say your want is to 'buy property', your reality is that 'I don't have property or enough money to buy now', and your roadblocks are 'I don't understand the buying process' and 'I suck at saving money so I'm not confident about committing to a mortgage'. In this case, you'd check whether you're missing any roadblocks by asking yourself, 'If I was better at saving, and was confident in my spending plan and how much I'd be able to put towards paying a mortgage, AND I understood the property buying process, would I be ready to buy?'

If the answer is yes, you've got all the roadblocks. If not, there's another roadblock you haven't identified yet. Figure out what it is and put it on your hit-list.

Making it happen

You've now listed out all the results you want, acknowledged your reality today, and created a super-focused list of your roadblocks. Now it's time to turn your roadblocks list into a list of action items.

Here's how you do this:

- First, go through your list of results and identify the ones that are most important to you.
- Next, look at the roadblocks that relate specifically to these results. (It's totally normal to have some overlap in these roadblocks.)
- If any roadblocks show up in a few places and impact more than one of your wants, write them on a roadblock hit-list.
- Use this hit-list to get clear on your priority actions and keep yourself moving towards the results you want.
- Then start taking the actions on this hit-list to clear your roadblocks and help you get from where you are now (your reality) to the outcomes you want (results).

Always start with the lowest-hanging fruit—a roadblock that's easy to clear while still making a big impact on being able to get the results you want. Pick this roadblock and set up an action plan to clear it. Don't try to tackle ten things at once: if you do, it's easy to become overwhelmed and give up. Instead, pick one roadblock, clear it, then move on to the next one.

Clearing this one roadblock will create a 'win' that will make you feel as though you're making progress. I can't emphasise enough how important this is to maintain your motivation and keep you moving forward toward the things you want. When I take people through this process, I always try to help them choose low-hanging fruit to clear. This gives them a feeling of progress and keeps their energy up as they work toward the next thing.

Follow this process and your momentum will build steadily over time as you clear more of your roadblocks, and tick off more of your wants or results.

Set a timeline to take action

It's so easy to get distracted and end up off track. Don't fall into this trap. The process above will work, but only if you act on it. Your money success is important, so prioritise to make it happen.

If you need someone to push you, link up with an accountability buddy or think about getting a Financial Adviser or Money Coach. Remember: the money you invest in paying someone will pay for itself *many* times over through much better money outcomes over time. You'll also have more clarity in your direction and more confidence in the action you're taking. Those are things I think everyone should have: things that are so valuable you can't put a price on them.

Whatever you want, take the action to make it happen.

PUTTING IT ALL TOGETHER

The Reality, Roadblocks, and Results exercise will help you get clear on what's important to you, where you're at now, and what's holding you back that you need to work through to get the things you want.

When you use it in relation to your specific goals and then go through the key money areas covered in this book (Structure, Strategy and Solutions), you'll cover the most critical areas you need to consider to create a life not limited by money.

This isn't the total solution, because money success doesn't just happen on its own. But this process will give you a clear list of action items you can step through to deliver the results you want from your money over time.

Then, once you've got your hit-list together, you need to make it happen. Set reminders on your phone, create calendar events, or do whatever you need to do to keep your focus on your hit-list along your journey to money success.

If you need to get some help to bust through the roadblocks that are standing in your way, do it.

I believe true money success—a life not limited by money—is possible for everyone who's prepared to commit and put in the work. But it won't just magically happen. Your results are driven by your motivation and commitment to taking the action needed to get the results you want.

In the end, the choice is yours.

Take action with confidence

This book gives you the plan and steps to Get Unstuck, but ideas without action are worthless. To make your next steps easier, I've put together some free training where I'll personally guide you through implementing the learnings from the book so you can fast-track your results.

Scan the code below to unlock this training for free:

What's the next step?

Every person deserves to live a life not limited by money.

I believe it's something that's possible for anyone who's prepared to commit to making it happen.

The journey can be complex, but the destination is absolutely worth it. I want you to use this book as a launch pad to getting the money results you need to create the lifestyle you want.

But to do that, you need to take ACTION.

Hopefully this book has given you the tools, knowledge, and motivation to help you get started.

But it's often hard to do it on your own. Having the right help with your finances will allow you to shortcut your way to money success. It will provide a solid framework that will give you the confidence to take action, and make sure you avoid roadblocks and momentum-killing mistakes along the way.

If you need help, please feel free to reach out. You can contact me through the Pivot Wealth website at www.pivotwealth.com.au.

I also run financial education workshops and events, and produce money content to help build your money IQ and push you forward financially. Find out more at www.pivotwealth.com.au.

To your success.

Ben

Bibliography

Chapter 1

Baumeister, Roy. 2011. *Willpower: Rediscovering the greatest human strength*. Penguin Press.

Thaler, Richard H. and Sunstein, Cass. 2008. *Nudge*. Yale University Press.

Wansink, Brian. 2006. *Mindless eating: Why we eat more than we think*. Bantam Press.

Chapter 2

Covey, Steven. 2018. *The 7 habits of highly effective people*. Simon & Schuster.

Kahneman, Daniel. 2012. *Thinking fast and slow*. Farrar, Straus & Giroux Inc.

Nofsinger, John R. 2012. *The psychology of investing*. Routledge.

Chapter 3

Ferris, Tim. 2016. *Tools of Titans*. Ebury Publishing.

Schwartz, Barry. 2017. *The Paradox of Choice: why more is less*. Ecco Press.

Chapter 7

Chu, Melissa. August, 2017. *Research Reveals That Publicly Announcing Your Goals Makes You Less Likely to Achieve Them* - https://www.inc.com/melissa-chu/announcing-your-goals-makes-you-less-likely-to-ach.html (retrieved June 2018)

Diamond, Dan. January, 2013. *Just 8% of People Achieve Their New Year's Resolutions. Here's How They Do It* - https://www.forbes.com/sites/dandiamond/2013/01/01/just-8-of-people-achieve-their-new-years-resolutions-heres-how-they-did-it/#17f06716596b (retrieved June 2018)

Evans, Lisa. June, 2015. *Why Sharing Your Progress Makes You More Likely To Accomplish Your Goals* - https://www.fastcompany.com/3047432/why-sharing-your-progress-makes-you-more-likely-to-accomplish-your-goals (retrieved June 2018)

Schwantes, Marcel. July, 2016. *Science Says 92 Percent of People Don't Achieve Their Goals. Here's How the Other 8 Percent Do* - https://www.inc.com/marcel-schwantes/science-says-92-percent-of-people-dont-achieve-goals-heres-how-the-other-8-perce.html (retrieved June 2018)

Wissman, Barrett. March, 2018. *An Accountability Partner Makes You Vastly More Likely to Succeed* - https://www.entrepreneur.com/article/310062 (retrieved June 2018)

Chapter 10

Richards, Carl. 2012. *The behaviour gap.* Penguin Press.

Rowley, James J. Jr., Walker, David J., and Ning, Sarinie Yating. 2018. *The case for low-cost index-fund investing.* Vanguard. https://static.vgcontent.info/crp/intl/auw/docs/literature/The-Case-for-Indexing-Australia.pdf (Retrieved June 2018)

Chapter 11

Curtin, Melanie. 2016. In an 8-*hour day, the average worker is productive for this many hours*. https://www.inc.com/melanie-curtin/in-an-8-hour-day-the-average-worker-is-productive-for-this-many-hours.html (retrieved June 2018)

News.com. 2017. *Employees average two hours and 53 minutes work a day, survey shows*. http://www.news.com.au/finance/work/at-work/employees-average-two-hours-and-53-minutes-work-a-day-survey-shows/news-story/16e8136e776adb98faccd407433249a8 (retrieved June 2018)

Chapter 12

Oliver, Shane. June, 2017. *The Australian economy hits another rough patch - implications for investors*. http://www.ampcapital.com.au/article-detail?alias=/olivers-insights/june-2017/australian-economy-another-rough-patch (Retrieved June, 2018)

Ross, Clare. 2017. *Superannuation account balances by age and gender*. ASFA research. https://www.superannuation.asn.au/ArticleDocuments/359/1710_Superannuation_account_balances_by_age_and_gender.pdf.aspx? (Retrieved June, 2018)